$750

AF569559

# Starting Out in Pastel

with Ken Goldman

Walter Foster

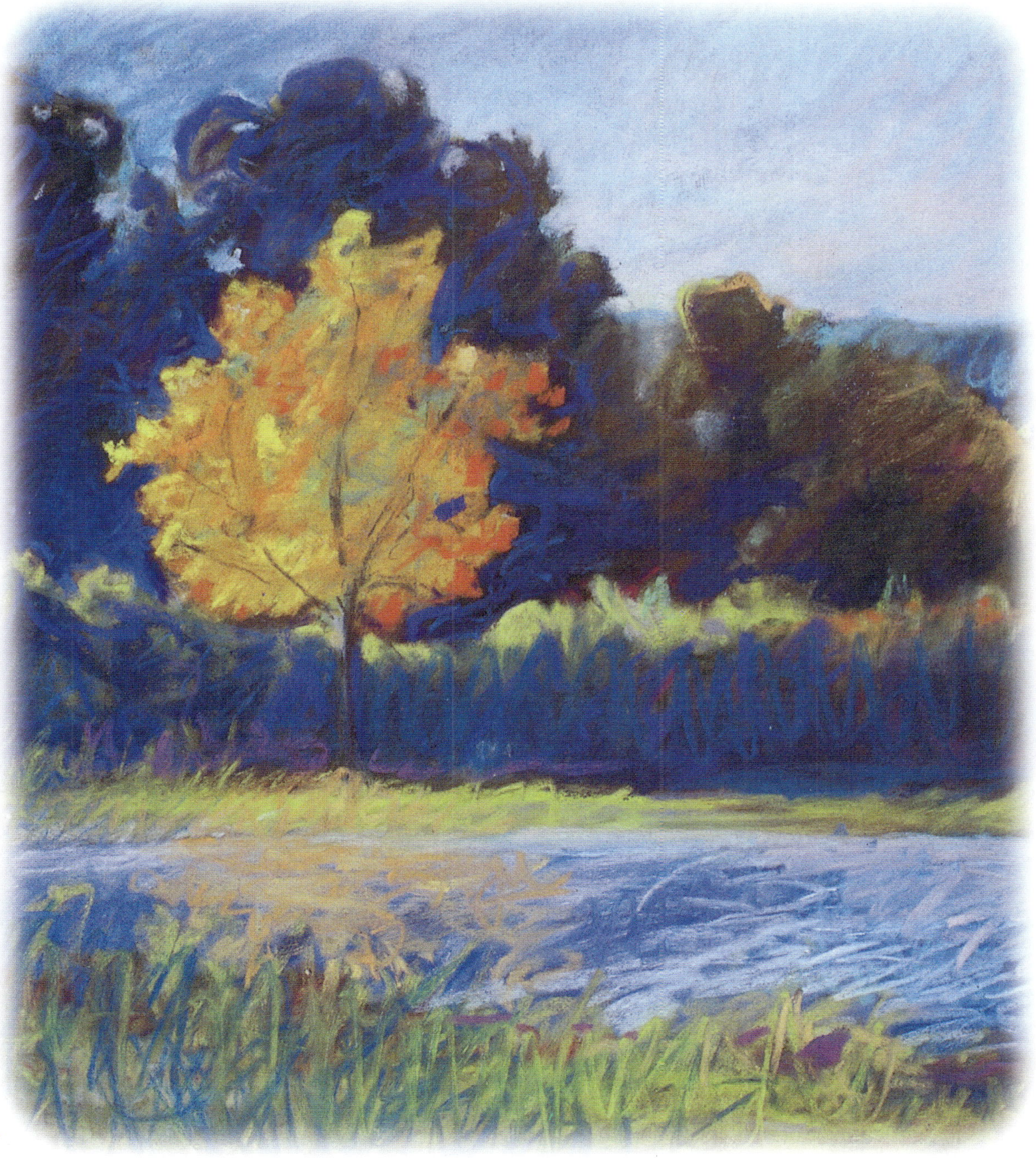

Pastel is an ideal painting and drawing medium. There are almost no technical aspects to master; it is very direct; it has glowing colors with exquisite textures; and, best of all, it is dry. This last feature makes pastel one of the most permanent of all painting media: the colors will not fade, yellow, or crack over time. So, when properly cared for, pastel paintings are as vibrant after 200 years as when they were originally rendered.

My goal in this book is to inspire you with a wide variety of pastel techniques and finished paintings. I hope you will study my approach, try copying a few pieces, and add what you learn to your own works. Then you'll be ready for the next book in this series, *Step-by-Step Pastel*. Remember, there's nothing like careful observation and practice to help you open your eyes and expand your artistic horizons!

Ken Goldman

## Contents

# Materials Make a Difference

ONE OF THE WONDERFUL things about pastel is that you don't need a lot of equipment and fancy tools; all you really need is a good set of colors and a surface to draw on. It's also a very "hands-on" kind of medium; nothing works as well for blending the colors as your own fingers! However, over the years, I have found a few tricks and extra tools that are particularly useful, which I will share with you here. You will soon develop your own preferences, but the materials on these pages will certainly get you off to a good start.

## Pastel Sets

Pastels come in a huge range of glowing colors, and you can get them in sticks and pencils—individually or in sets. I recommend sets for beginners; they are a good introduction to the colors available, and you can decide for yourself which colors you like best. In the studio, I keep both hard and soft pastels on hand, but on location, I take a set of 96 hard pastels. It has a good selection of colors, and it's small and light enough to carry easily. In general, though, I use hard pastels to lay in broad areas of color, and save the more expensive, but brilliant, soft pastels for finishing the painting.

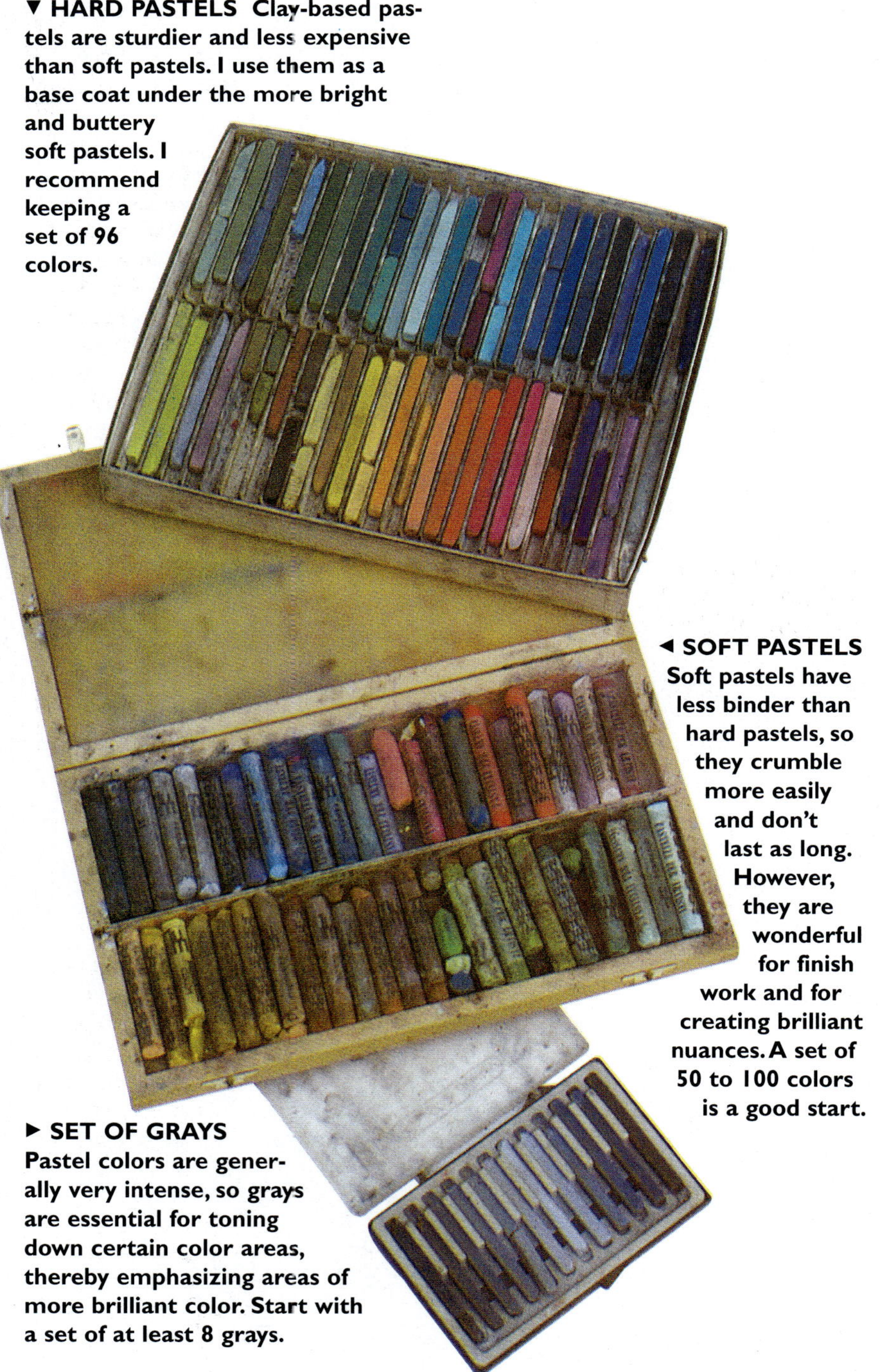

▼ **HARD PASTELS** Clay-based pastels are sturdier and less expensive than soft pastels. I use them as a base coat under the more bright and buttery soft pastels. I recommend keeping a set of 96 colors.

◀ **SOFT PASTELS** Soft pastels have less binder than hard pastels, so they crumble more easily and don't last as long. However, they are wonderful for finish work and for creating brilliant nuances. A set of 50 to 100 colors is a good start.

▶ **SET OF GRAYS** Pastel colors are generally very intense, so grays are essential for toning down certain color areas, thereby emphasizing areas of more brilliant color. Start with a set of at least 8 grays.

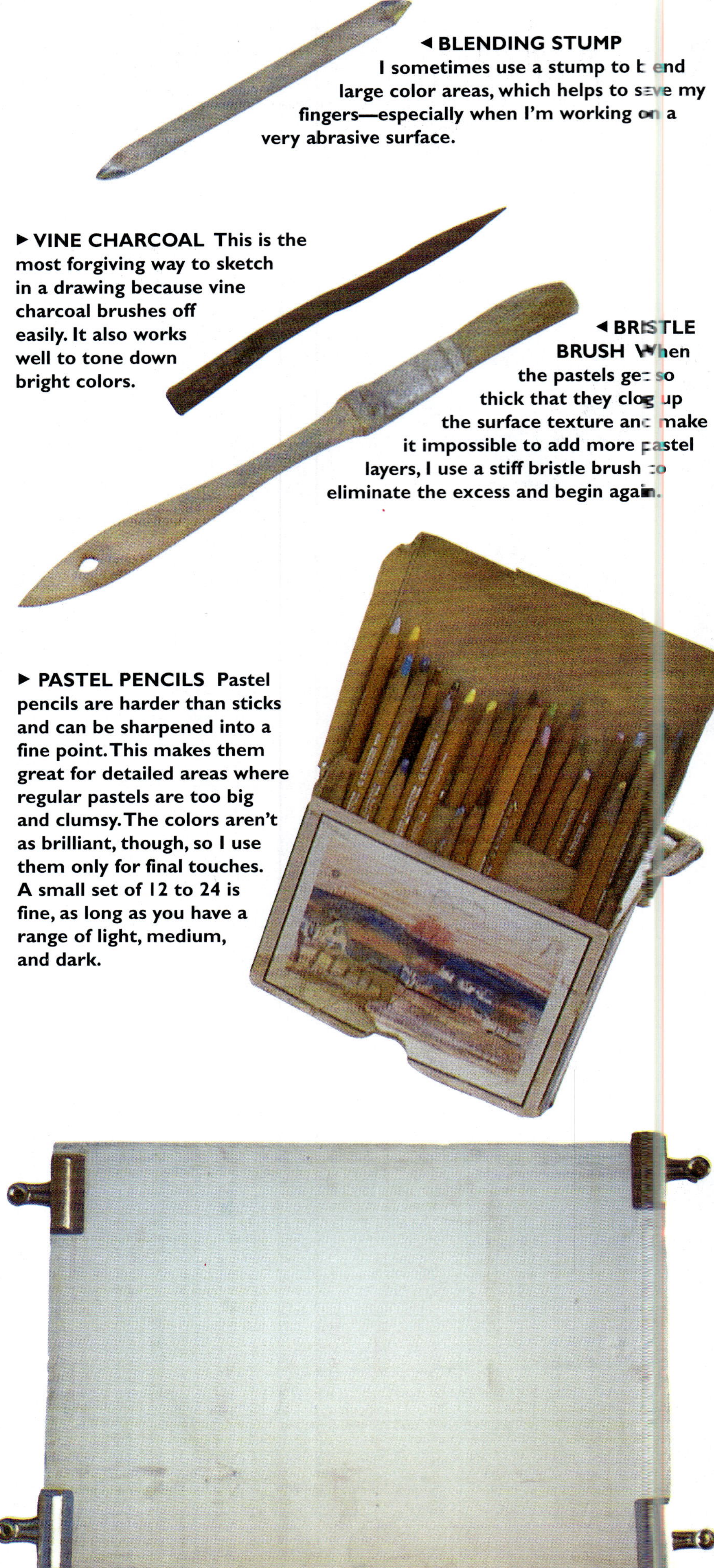

◀ **BLENDING STUMP** I sometimes use a stump to blend large color areas, which helps to save my fingers—especially when I'm working on a very abrasive surface.

▶ **VINE CHARCOAL** This is the most forgiving way to sketch in a drawing because vine charcoal brushes off easily. It also works well to tone down bright colors.

◀ **BRISTLE BRUSH** When the pastels get so thick that they clog up the surface texture and make it impossible to add more pastel layers, I use a stiff bristle brush to eliminate the excess and begin again.

▶ **PASTEL PENCILS** Pastel pencils are harder than sticks and can be sharpened into a fine point. This makes them great for detailed areas where regular pastels are too big and clumsy. The colors aren't as brilliant, though, so I use them only for final touches. A small set of 12 to 24 is fine, as long as you have a range of light, medium, and dark.

## Drawing Board and Portfolio

I use a combination drawing board and storage portfolio made of two pieces of foam-core board, 1 inch larger all around than the size of my pastel paper. I tape the board pieces together on one of their long sides and attach metal clips to hold my paper in place. This makes a great lightweight, portable support to work on with a place for storing paper and finished pastels.

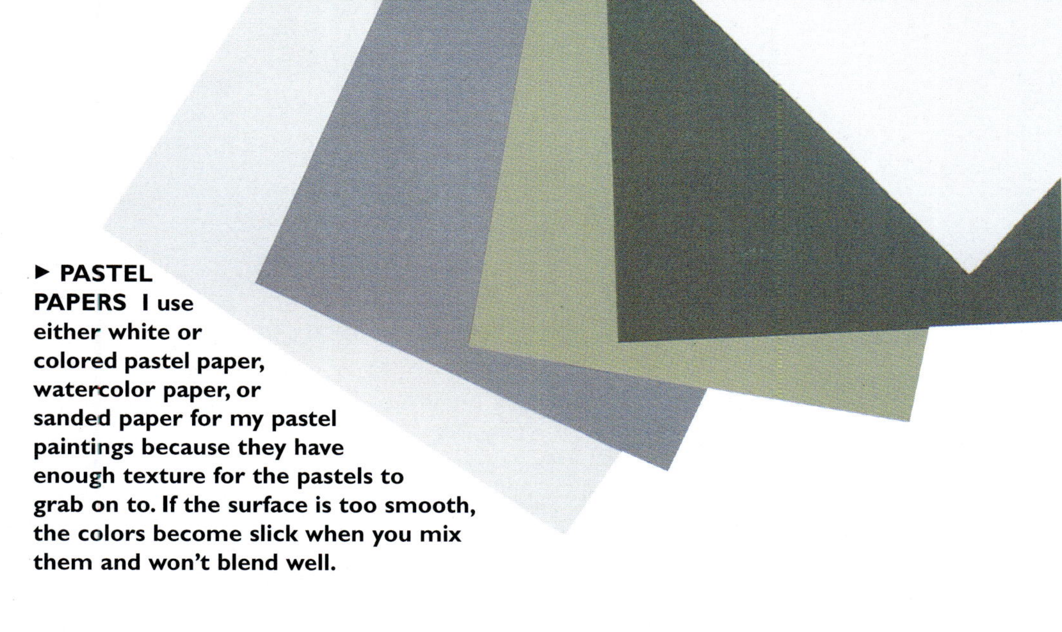

▶ **PASTEL PAPERS** I use either white or colored pastel paper, watercolor paper, or sanded paper for my pastel paintings because they have enough texture for the pastels to grab on to. If the surface is too smooth, the colors become slick when you mix them and won't blend well.

## Painting Surface

Unlike moist paints, pastels aren't mixed on a palette and then applied to canvas; instead, you mix the colors right on the painting surface itself. To stand up to all that color blending, you need a surface that is somewhat abrasive, so the colors have some "tooth" to stick to. For most paintings, I use middle-toned green, gray, or brown pastel paper. When I use white watercolor or sanded paper, I underpaint the dark areas first.

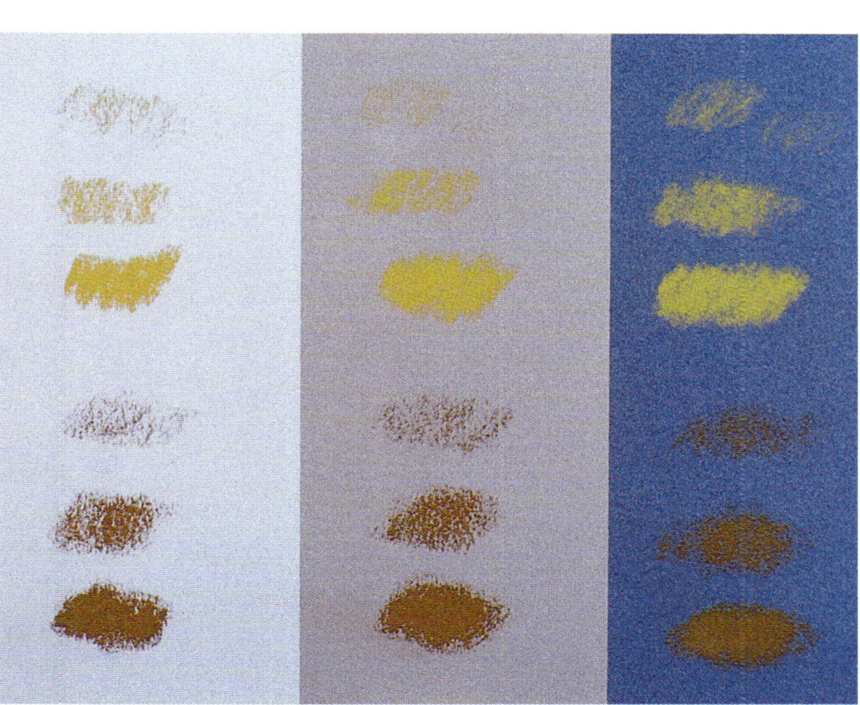

◀ **COLORED PAPERS** I often use colored papers because their existing middle tone allows me to quickly lay in extremes of dark and light—the essence of a strong visual statement. In these samples, I let a lot of the paper show through to demonstrate how it harmonizes with the pastel colors.

### Artist's Tip

*We call it "painting" in pastel, as well as drawing, because you mix the colors just as you would with paints. The difference is that you mix them on the paper instead of on a palette.*

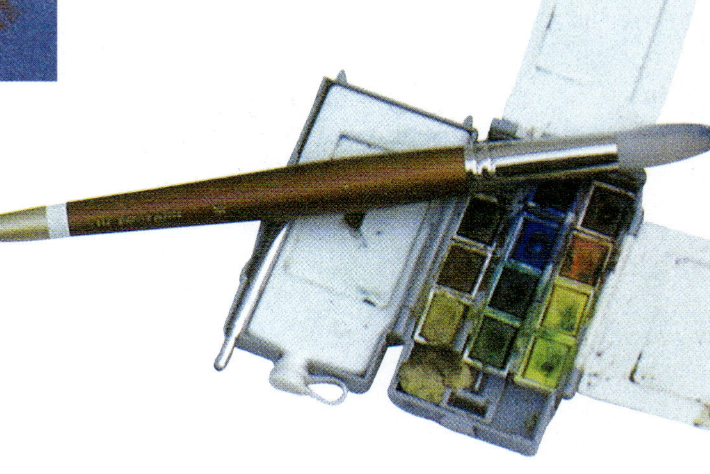

◀ **WATERCOLOR** When I use white watercolor paper, canvas, or sanded paper (a type that won't buckle), I like to underpaint my dark areas in watercolor first. This saves on expensive dark pastels and makes a toned ground to work on.

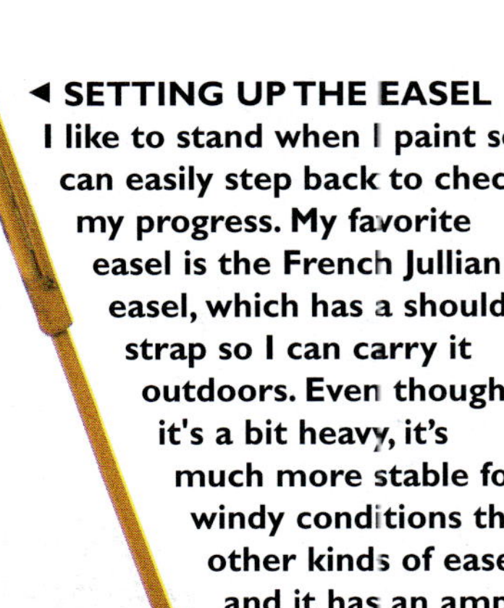

◀ **SETTING UP THE EASEL** I like to stand when I paint so I can easily step back to check my progress. My favorite easel is the French Jullian easel, which has a shoulder strap so I can carry it outdoors. Even though it's a bit heavy, it's much more stable for windy conditions than other kinds of easels, and it has an ample storage area.

## Razor Blades

I use razor blades to sharpen a point on hard pastels and pastel pencils or to score soft pastels before breaking them into two pieces. To sharpen a pastel, rest the unnumbered end on a firm support and shape it with a razor blade while rotating the stick.

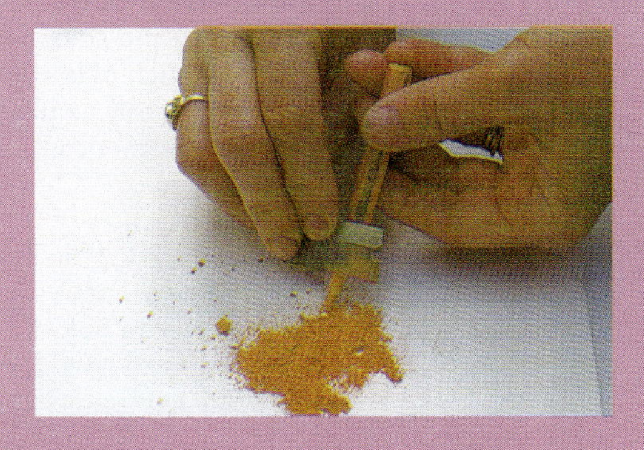

▲ **SPRAY FIXATIVE** Fixative is generally used to set a finished painting and keep the colors from smudging, but it has a tendency to darken colors. I sometimes use fixative to deliberately darken certain areas or to permanently fix a charcoal underdrawing, but I seldom, if ever, use fixative at the end.

# Starting with Values

THE FIRST STEP toward a beautiful pastel painting is an underdrawing of values—black, white, and the shades of gray in between. It's easy for beginners to get carried away and want to start painting immediately with a rainbow of colors. Even experienced pastelists sometimes sacrifice strong lights and darks for exciting color, and the result is that they end up with neither. Instead, I apply color on top of a solid light and dark underdrawing. You'll find it much easier to draw when you aren't distracted by choosing colors as well as values right off the bat.

### Making a Charcoal Underdrawing

I often use vine charcoal for my underdrawing. Vine charcoal is an ideal medium to use under pastels because it produces very strong light, medium, and dark values; it wipes off easily when necessary; and it doesn't clog up the paper texture. These features make it easy to make accurate drawings before applying color. When I'm done with the drawing, I spray it heavily with fixative. This keeps it from smudging and prepares it for a pastel overpainting. For more information on drawing with charcoal, see my book titled *Charcoal Drawing* in Walter Foster's Artist's Library series.

## Painting from Photos

Photography allows you to freeze a moment in time, and you can learn a lot about rendering details by studying photographs (called *photo references*). I don't mean you should never paint from life; you can learn a lot by studying living, breathing nature. Still, images on photos don't move and the light doesn't shift, so you can take your time when painting from a photo. Plus, it's fun to combine parts from different photographs to create a work of art that is truly your own.

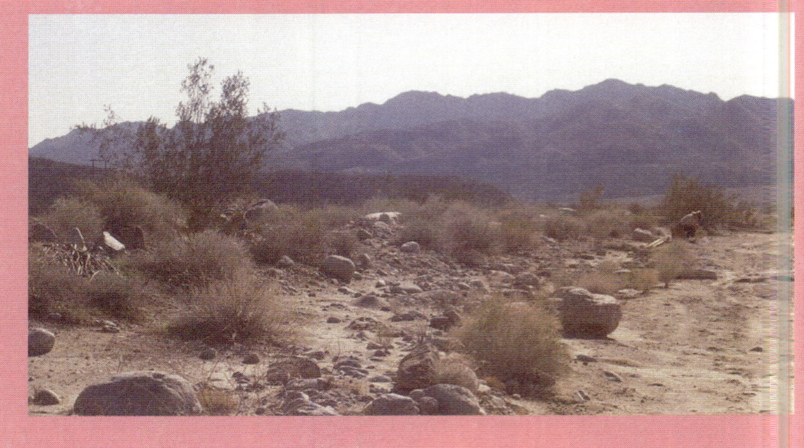

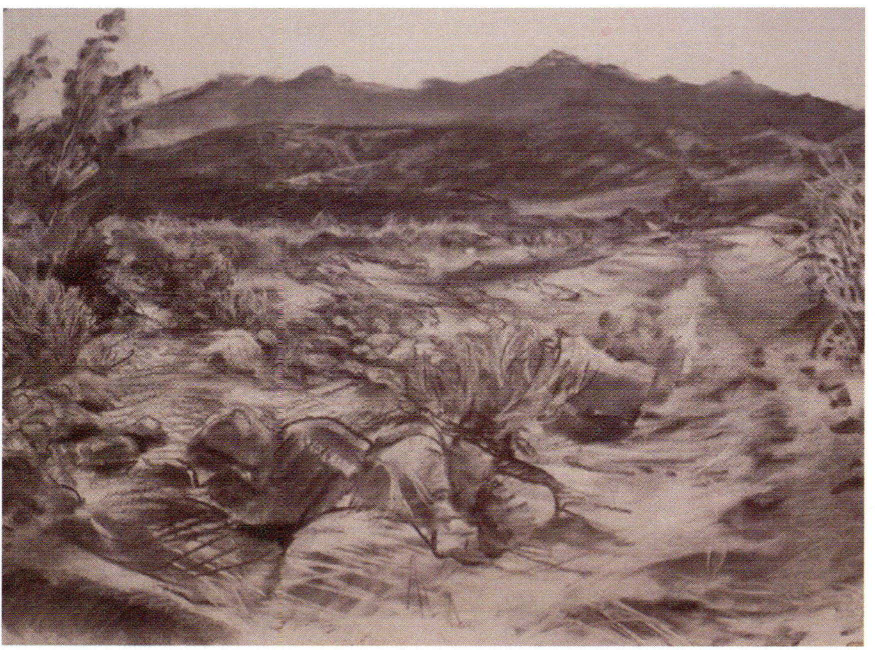

◄ **STARTING WITH CHARCOAL I made this underdrawing using vine charcoal on toned paper. Once I've sketched in the basic shapes of the elements, I can very quickly begin laying in the light, medium, and dark values simply by varying the pressure of my strokes. As you can see, charcoal leaves a fairly lightweight drawing, compared to the dense pastel underdrawing shown below, so it won't have as strong a toning effect on the final colors.**

### Creating a Base with Gray Pastels

When I'm going to paint a scene that has a lot of atmosphere—such as a misty valley or hazy, distant mountains—I use my small set of gray pastels for the underdrawing, instead of using charcoal. (See pages 6 and 7 for more on creating atmosphere.) The pastels have more substance and texture than charcoal, so when I add the color pastels on top, they mix right into the grays, creating soft, muted tones. This allows me to infuse a sense of atmosphere into the painting at the same time that I am establishing the important values. Try both methods of underpainting, and see the different results you achieve.

### Artist's Tip

*The amount of pressure you apply when painting with pastels influences the color's richness. Each color can yield up to three distinct values, depending on whether you use light, medium, or hard pressure.*

► **STARTING WITH GRAYS Here is an underdrawing done in gray pastels. With pastels, I use a variety of light, medium, and dark grays for the different values, whereas in charcoal, the tones are derived from changing the pressure on one stick of black. Compare this example to the charcoal drawing above. Charcoal leaves a very thin drawing under the final colors; gray pastels mix with the colors and become part of the finished painting.**

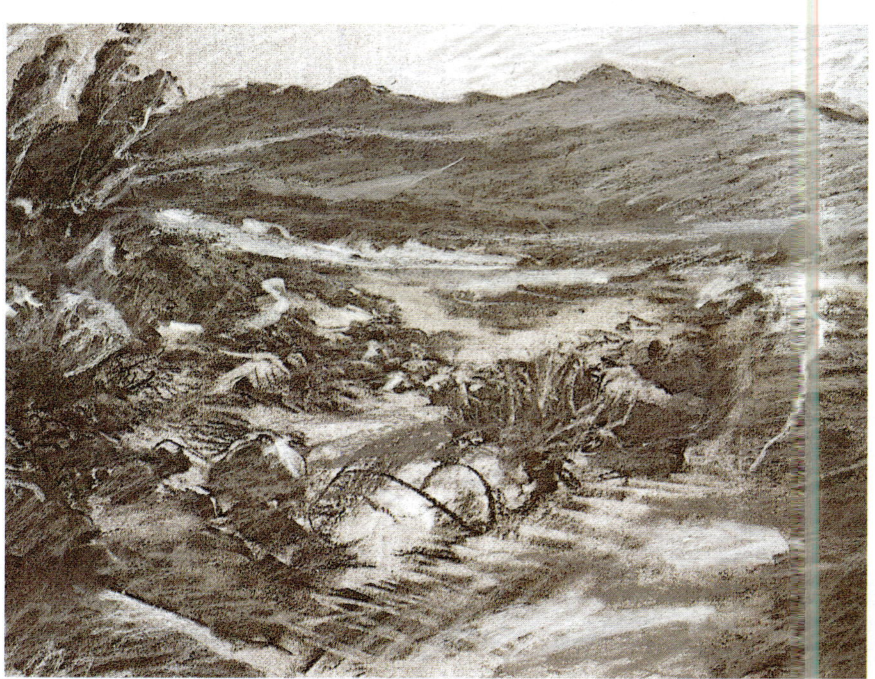

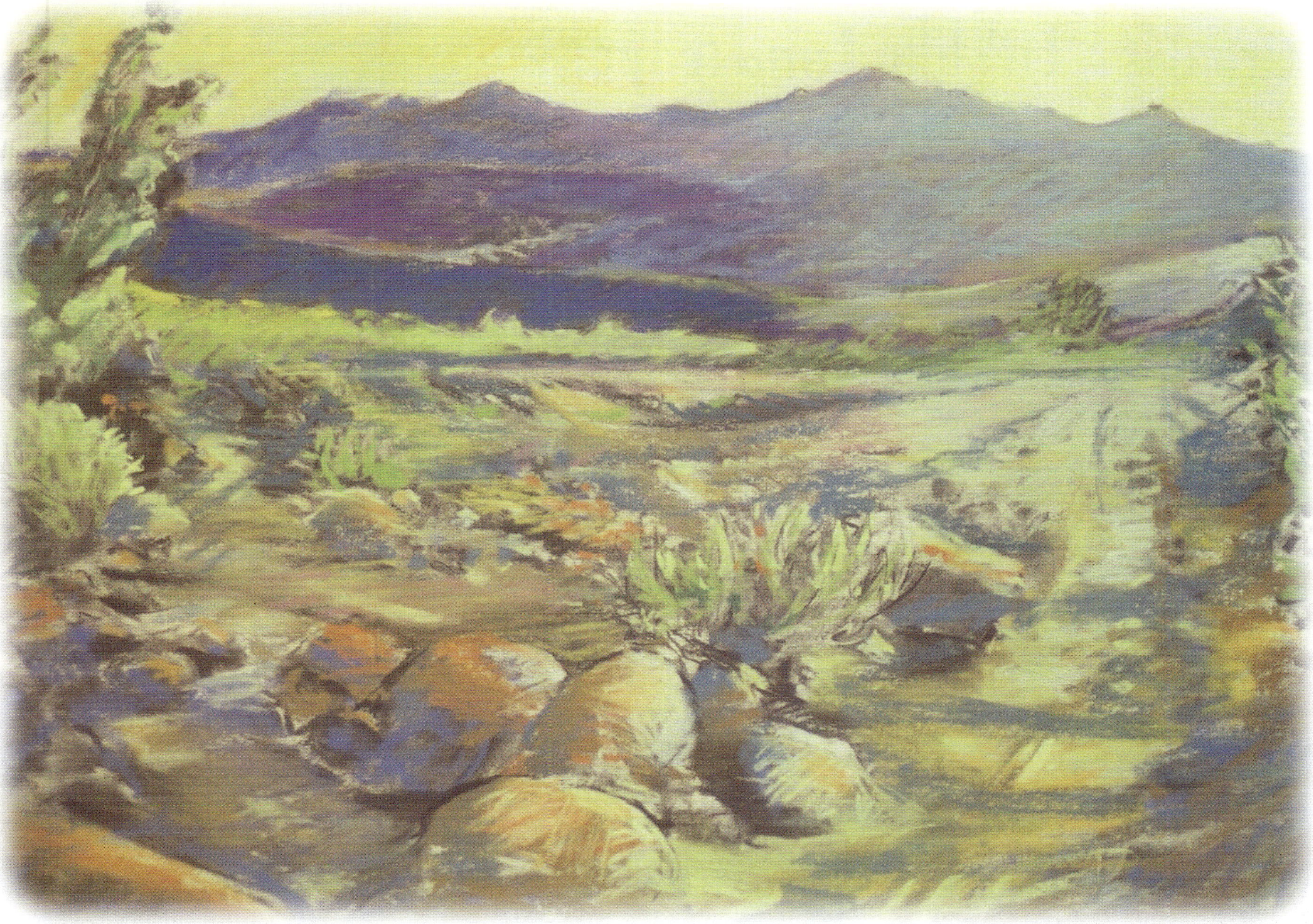

**DESERT PASTEL** **This finished pastel shows what a strong-value drawing beneath beautiful colors can do; it enriches the painting with depth and nuances.**

## Experimenting with Watercolor

Once you have a strong black, gray, and white value drawing, the color comes easily. I often use the charcoal drawing as a model for making separate watercolor studies so I can plan what colors should go where. In these quick "thumbnail" watercolors, I simply translate the light and dark values of gray into light and dark values of the various colors. Then I have all the direction I need for choosing colors in my final pastel, whether I want to paint right away or decide to wait until later.

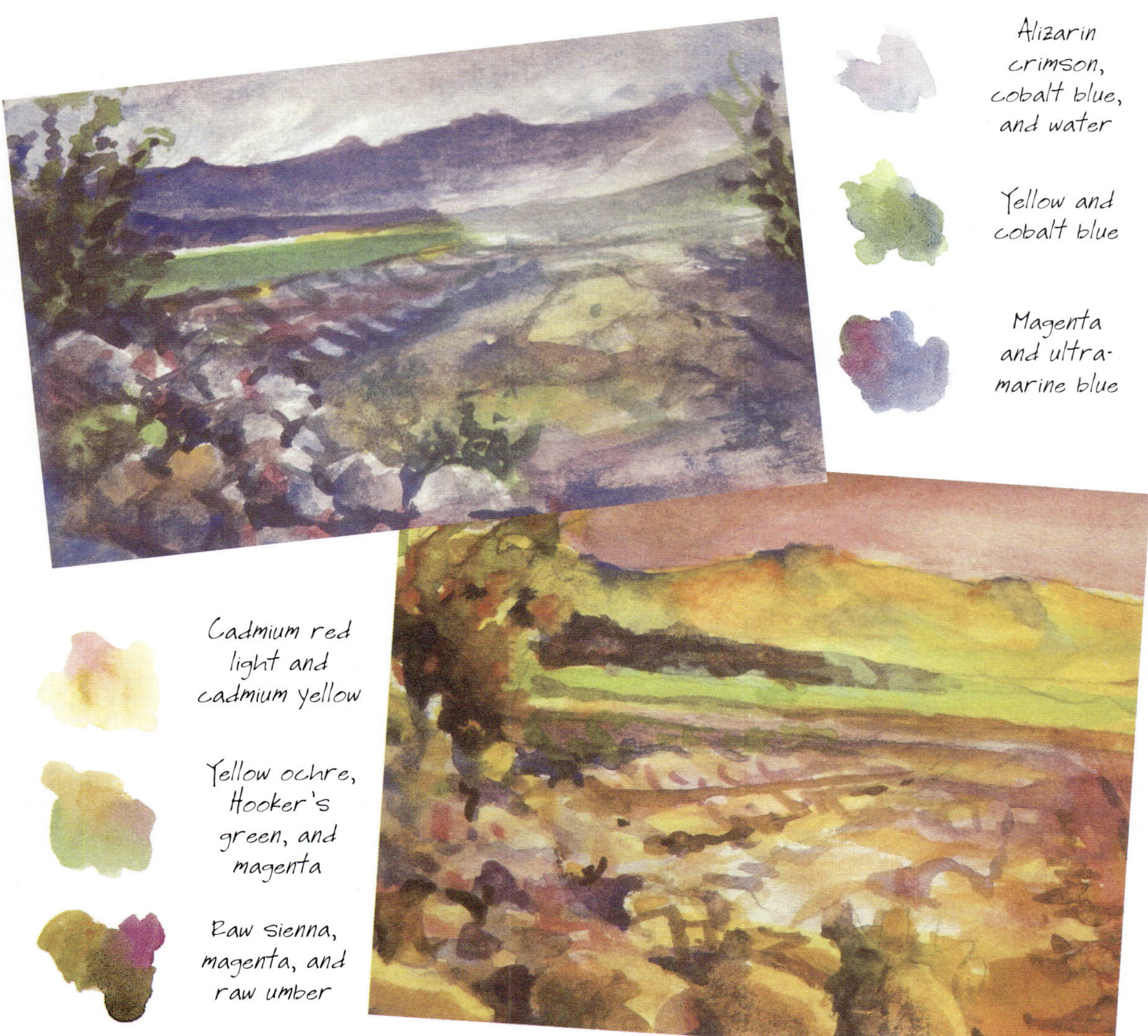


◂ **MAKING COLOR CHOICES** **These two 3" x 5" watercolor sketches were based on the initial charcoal drawing on page 4 and my imagination. As long as the values are correct, I can use any colors I want. I experimented with several color schemes before deciding on one to use as a guide for the pastel above.**

# Creating Lifelike Landscapes

ONE OF THE REASONS I ENJOY painting landscapes is meeting the challenge of creating the illusion of three dimensions on a flat surface. By manipulating color, overlapping objects, and emphasizing perspective, I can create a lifelike sense of depth and distance in my landscapes. It's fun to analyze a scene and decide what to focus on and how to rearrange the elements to make the viewer feel as if he or she were there.

### Generating a Sense of Depth

I use three different methods for creating dimension, and all are shown in the paintings on these pages. One method is to use *atmospheric* or *aerial perspective*, which refers to the way the moisture in the atmosphere makes forms in the distance look grayer, bluer, and more vague. A second method is to *overlap* objects, or make one object or area seem to recede by setting it behind another. The third technique is to apply *linear perspective*—a simple example is the way railroad tracks appear to narrow and then vanish into the distance.

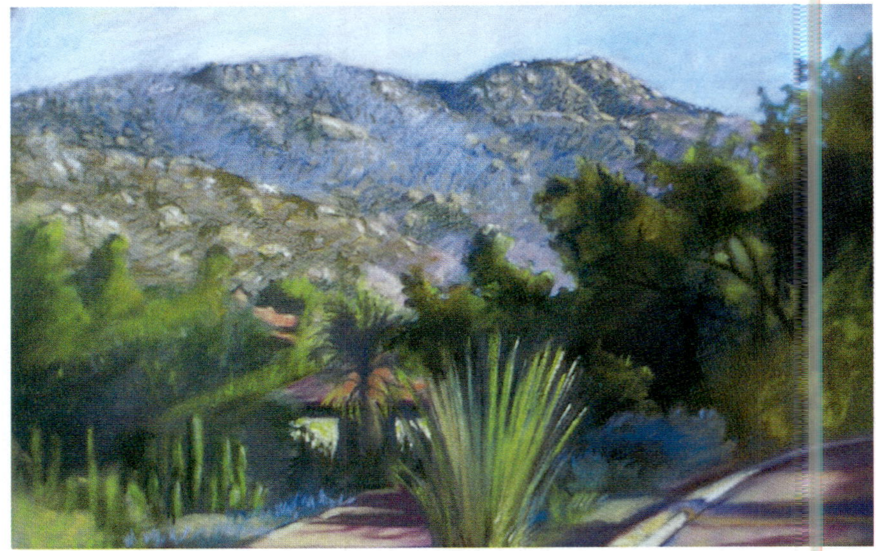

**OVERLAPPING** In this scene, I created a feeling of depth primarily by overlapping the elements. The tall foreground grass pushes the dark trees and light shack into the distance. They, in turn, overlap the first mountain, which then forces the farther peak into the background.

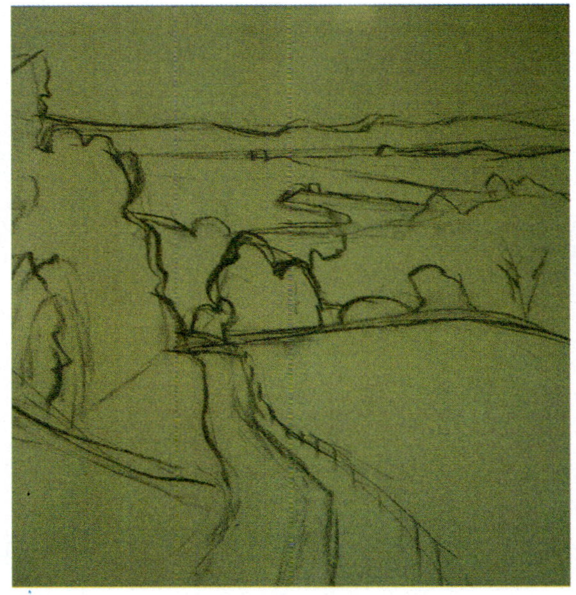

**CLARIFYING THE PERSPECTIVE** In this sketch, I altered the scene a bit to emphasize the receding parallel lines of the road. This sketch is only a starting guideline. My drawings are continually refined throughout the painting process, as the shapes are gradually developed with color.

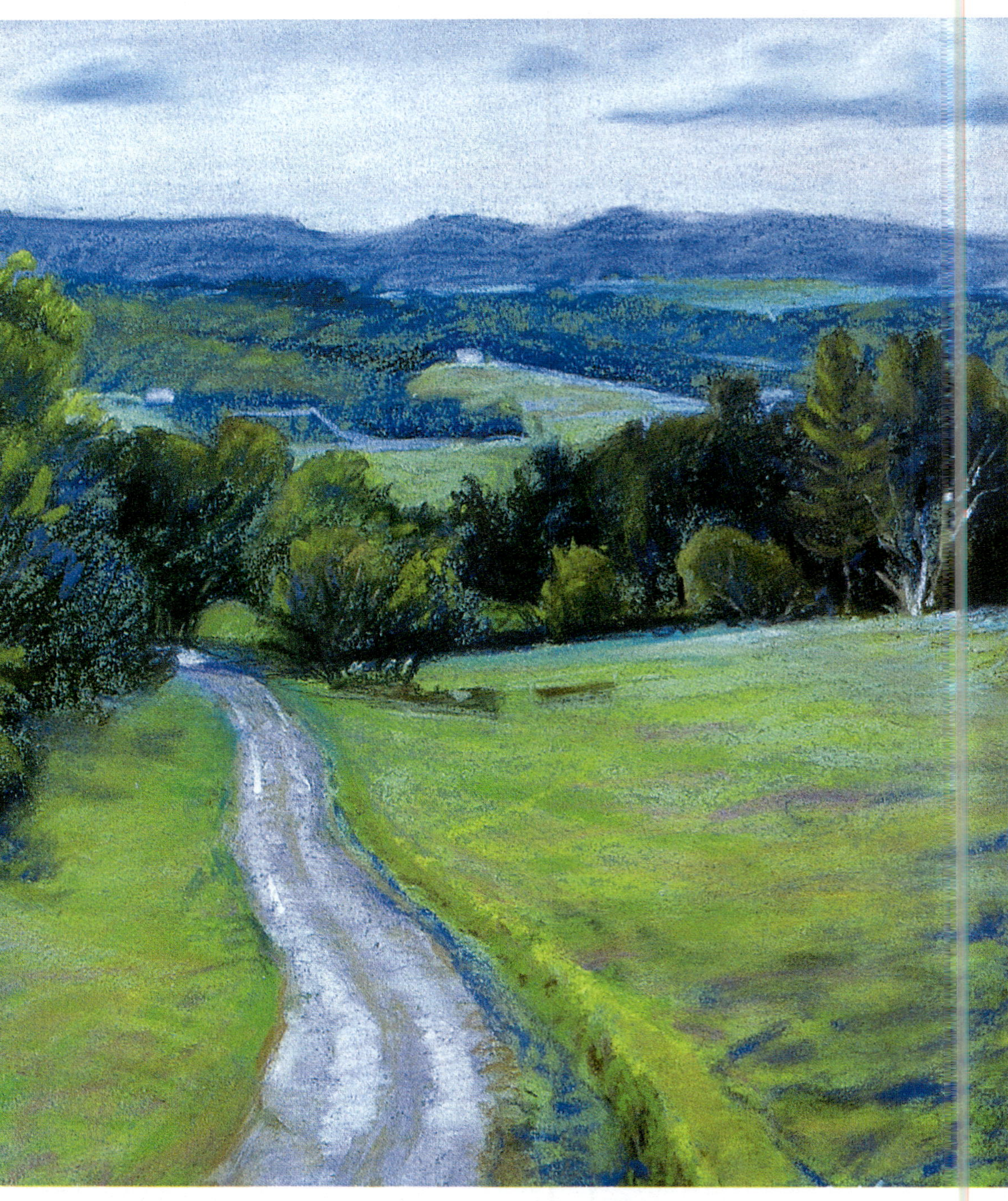

**LINEAR PERSPECTIVE** This is an example of linear perspective at work. As I developed the painting, I designed the distant field so it acted almost as a pointer to direct the eye back. I also reorganized the background forest into what looks like an orchard with directional lines. This gives the eye further reason to meander back toward the distant mountain range.

**Artist's Tip**

When traveling, I rely on watercolor to lay in basic colors and finish with a small set of pastels. Watercolor is cheaper and easier to replace than exotic pastel colors.

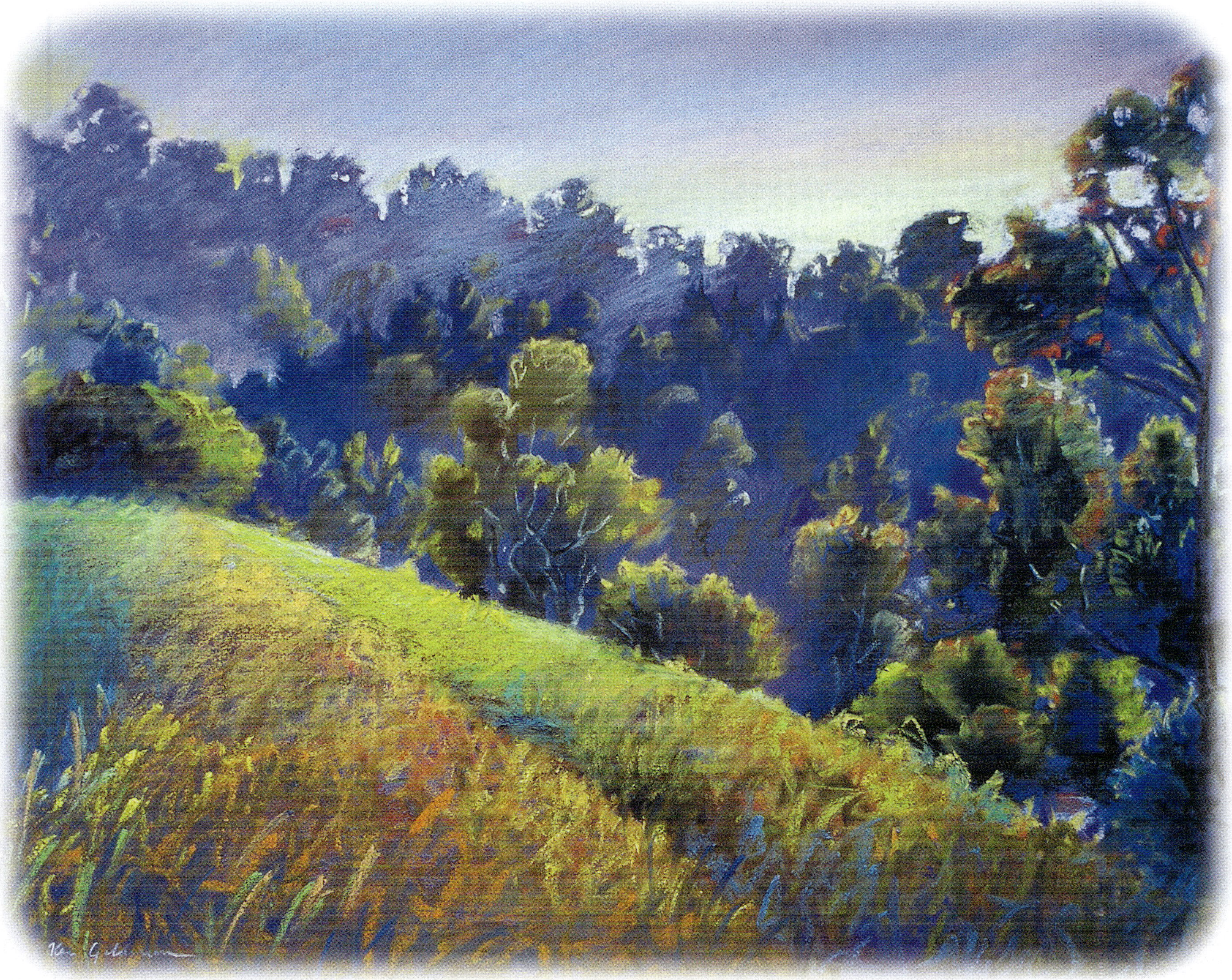

**AERIAL PERSPECTIVE** **Here I applied aerial perspective. The ocean mists make the distant trees bluer and hazier than the detailed, reddish foreground.**

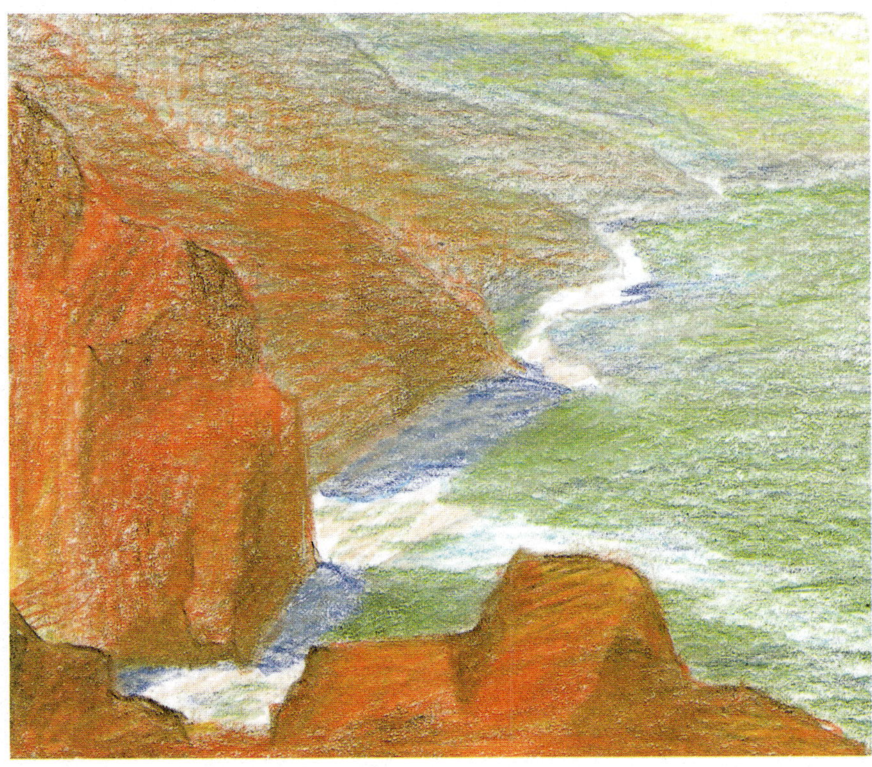

**CREATING ATMOSPHERE** **This is a quick thumbnail study showing in more detail how I infuse a sense of atmosphere through color. Notice how the red cliffs gradually become bluer and paler as they recede.**

## Redesigning a Scene

Although I may use photos as references to paint from, I don't like to feel tied to the particulars of a photo, especially if only a small part is interesting. Feel free to alter references as much as you like. Take a piece of paper and cover what doesn't interest you; lay tracing paper over what's left, and raise, lower, or remove parts that you would like to see changed. Try out a number of different possibilities until you find one that's pleasing to you. (My final version of this flower field is on page 15.)

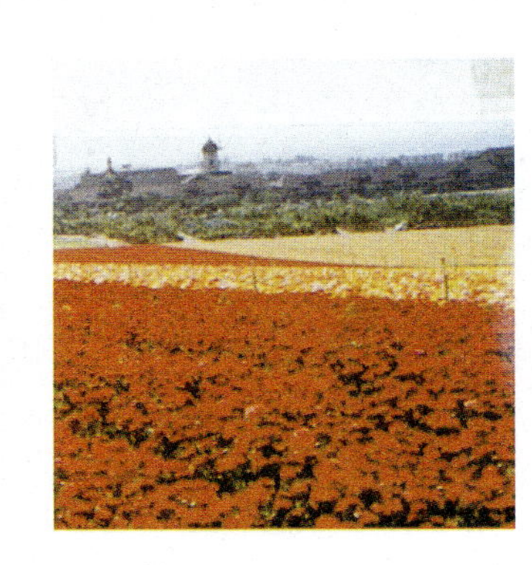

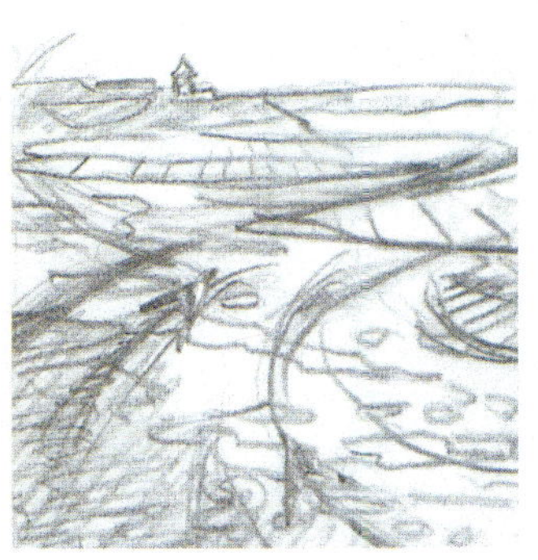

# Making Beautiful Still Lifes

A TIME-HONORED TRADITION of artists is to paint still lifes and interiors, and pastel colors with their subtle blends add richness to any indoor scene. I have a lot of admiration for the time involved in planning elegant setups, but my favorite approach is to look for everyday objects that are already assembled in interesting ways (and arrange one or two things a little). I then use a distinct light source that lifts the arrangement out of the ordinary and creates a distinct mood. I also make sure that my still lifes and interiors lead the viewer's eye into and around the painting on an exciting visual journey.

### Creating an Eye Path

The two pastels on this page were both essentially "found" arrangements—that is, I barely rearranged the elements. These paintings show what first caught my eye and made me want to paint them. Both have a definite focal point, strong design, repetition of diagonals and horizontals, varying textures, and contrasts of light against dark.

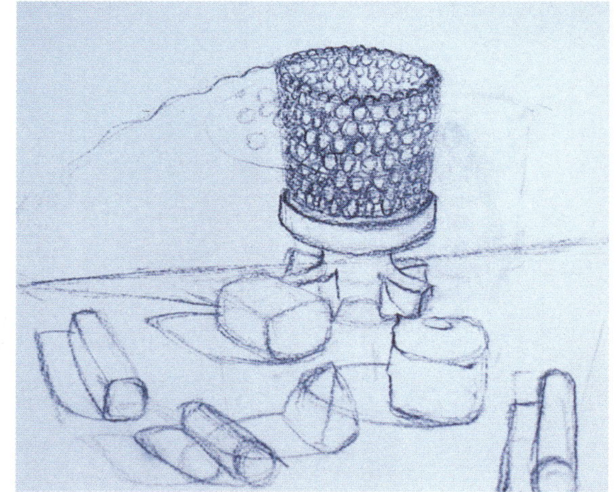

► **DRAWING THE SHAPES** **Here is a step-by-step demonstration of painting a still life over a value drawing. With vine charcoal on watercolor paper, I began by lightly sketching in the basic shapes and outlines. I particularly liked the way the placement of the pastel sticks added a sense of movement.**

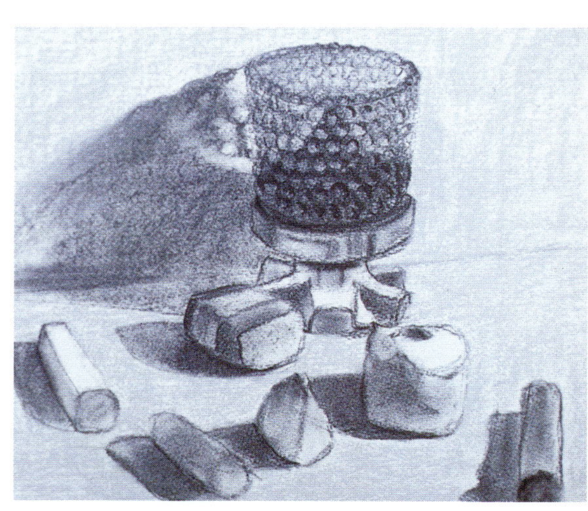

► **APPLYING GRAYS** **Using only gray hard pastels, I temporarily ignored color and gave my full attention to accurate drawing, light and dark values, and composition (the arrangement of objects and how they relate to each other in size and shape).**

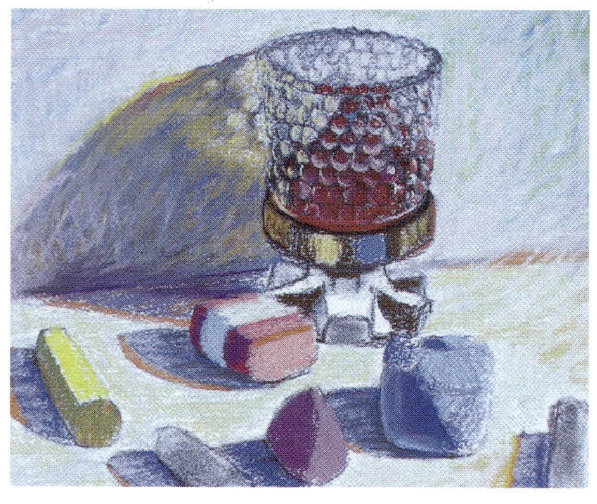

► **ADDING COLOR** **Then I started applying hard and soft pastel colors that had the same range of values as the underdrawing. I used light pressure on the pastel for the soft shadow on the wall, and increased the pressure for the dark areas in the glass, the pastels, and parts of the pastels' shadows.**

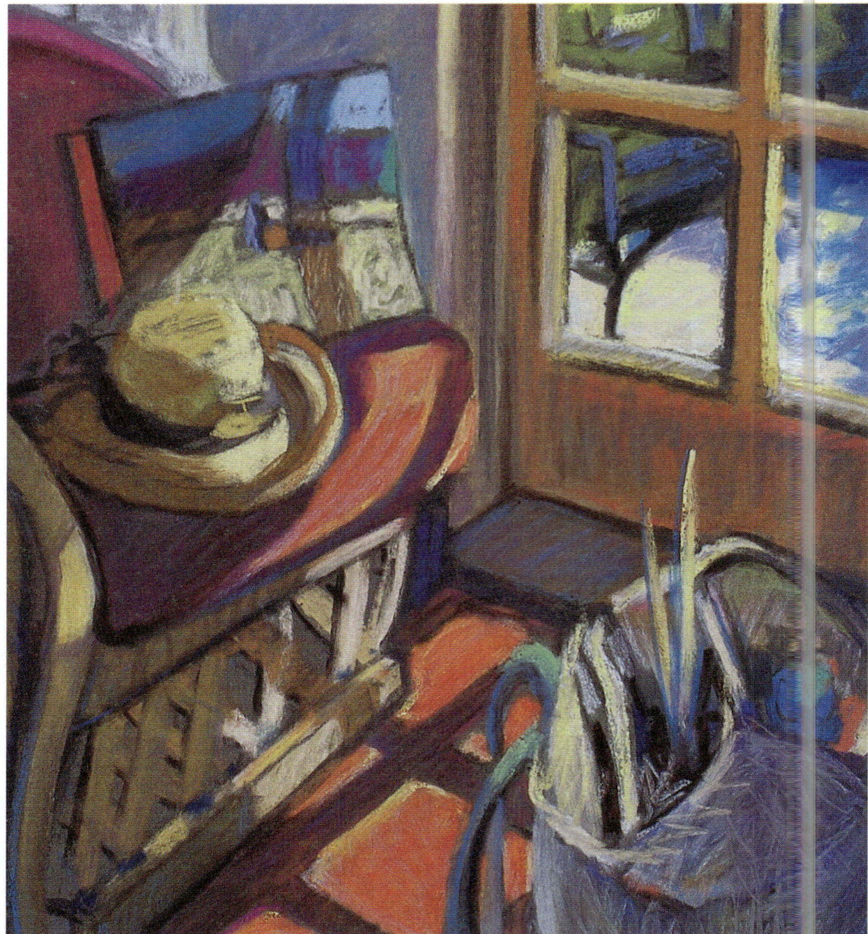

**INTERIOR WITH A HAT** **The pattern of the panes on the French door, the design of the shadow on the carpet, the diagonal lines in the wicker chair—all knit the elements together through the design principle called *repetition*. I also tried to keep the viewer engaged by employing a number of different contrasts—namely, lights against darks, smooth surfaces against textures, and bright colors against grays.**

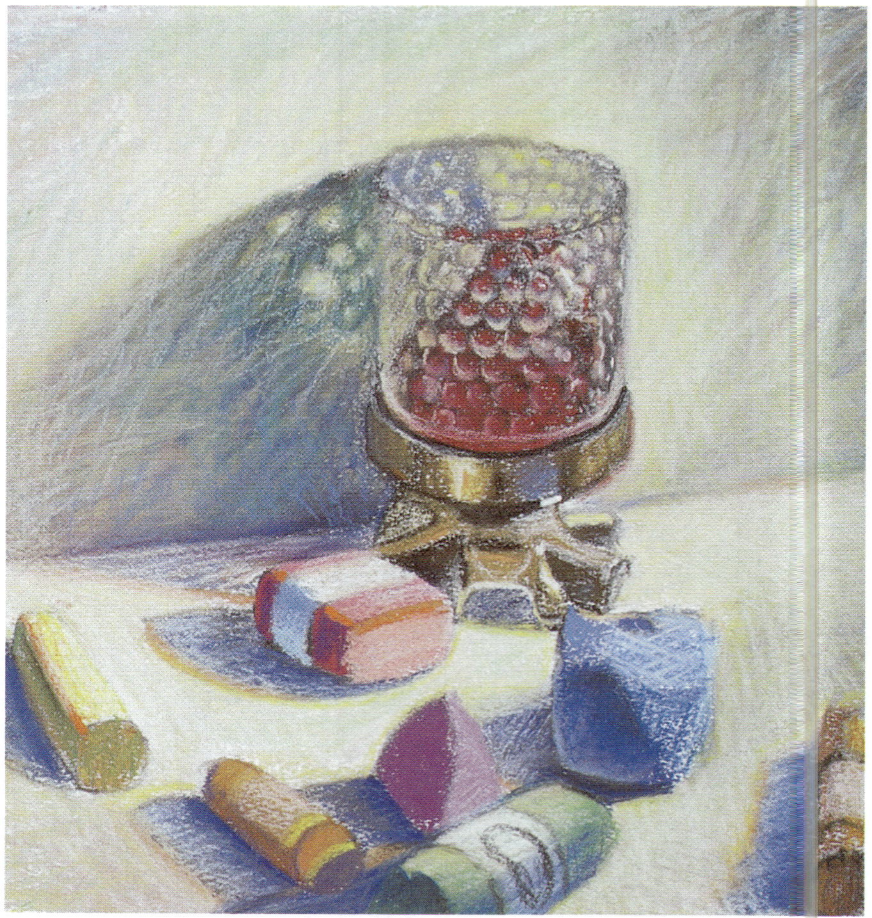

**CANDLE HOLDER** **You've probably noticed that once I started applying the pastel colors, I decided to add a green pastel stick to the bottom to make the foreground a little more interesting. It adds another opposing diagonal line that leads the viewer's eye through the composition and then points back toward the center of interest: the candle holder.**

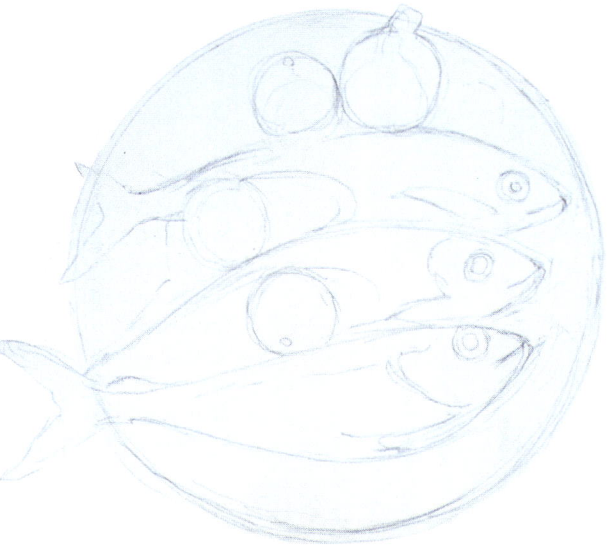

◂ **REPEATING SHAPES** The predominant design principle in this picture is repetition of shape—in the round plate, eyes, onion, and oranges—which I was able to accentuate by painting from a bird's-eye view of the whole arrangement.

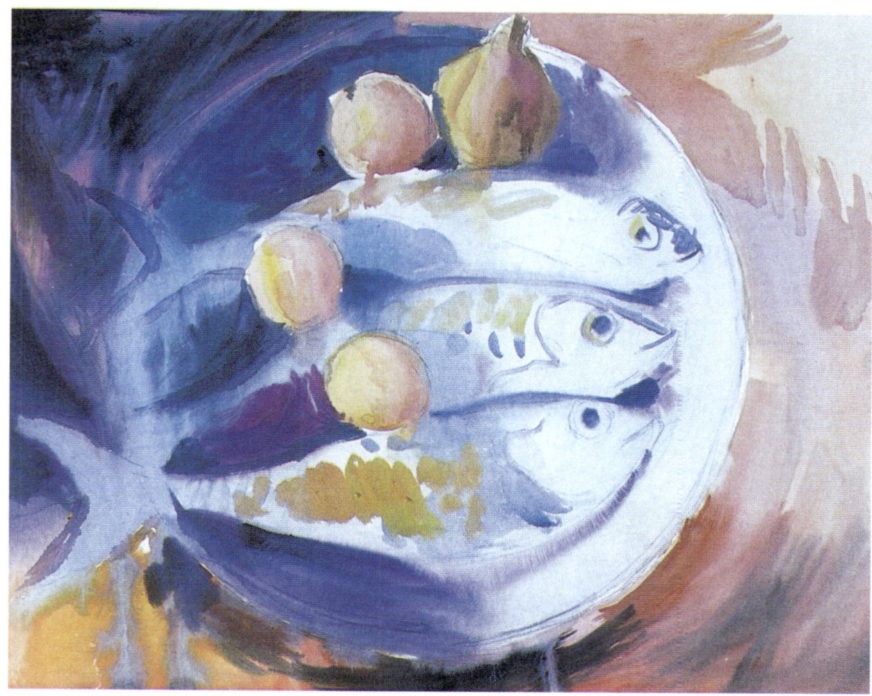

**USING CONTRASTS** For this still life, I chose a strong light source to highlight the fish (the focal point) and to create deep shadows for contrast. To set the value of the dark background corner, I started with black pastel and then softened the black with dark blues and browns. I also used a dark base of color—this time green—for the shadows on the fish. Then I continued developing the fish and mandarins using my soft pastels and choosing vibrant contrasts of orange and blue.

## Painting What Is Close at Hand

The interior scenes on these pages are proof that anything can be used to compose an interesting picture. In fact, the best part of painting something as mundane as this is the challenge of finding beauty in the ordinary. It's also great fun to look at your subject from an unusual viewpoint, as I did in *Fish and Mandarins*. There I placed the platter on the floor so the view would emphasize the round forms.

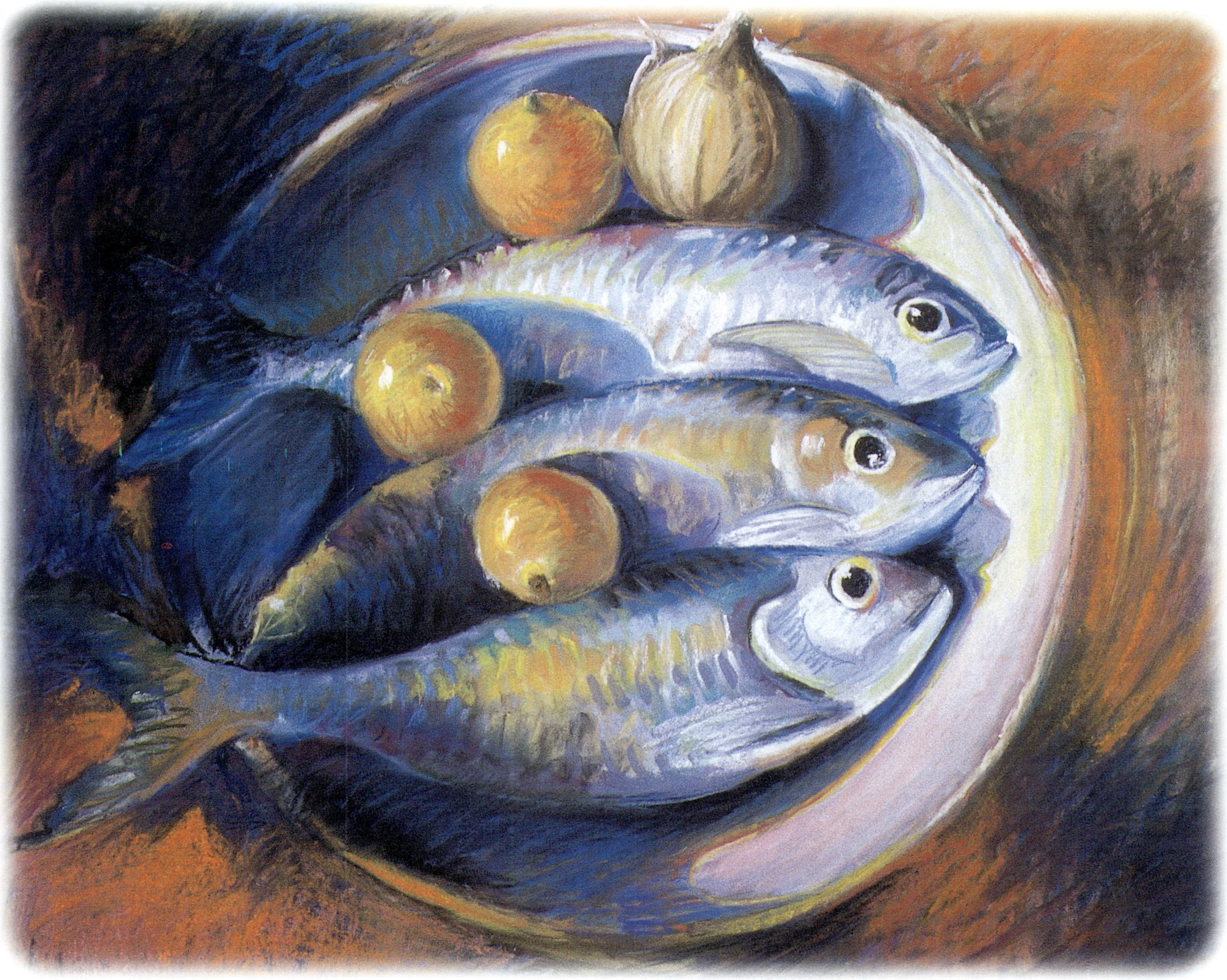

**FISH AND MANDARINS** To tie everything together visually, I repeated the orange colors of the mandarins in the background and on the fishes' scales.

# Painting Animals and Birds

I WAS PRIMARILY A WILDLIFE ARTIST from 1968 to 1980. After branching out into other art forms, I came to a realization that simplified everything for me: The key to painting any subject well is the ability to see it as an assembly of various values, colors, shapes, and textures—rather than as a specific thing. Try approaching painting animals this way. I think you will find it much easier than you may have thought!

### Drawing from Basic Shapes

Every good pastel starts with a good drawing, and every good drawing—whether it's of a landscape, still life, or your favorite pet—starts with simple shapes. Look carefully at your animal subject and break it down into a few basic shapes, such as ovals, circles, and wedges. Then gradually refine the lines and add more details. Follow the examples on this page, and practice drawing animals from photos or magazines—and from life, if you can get them to stay still!

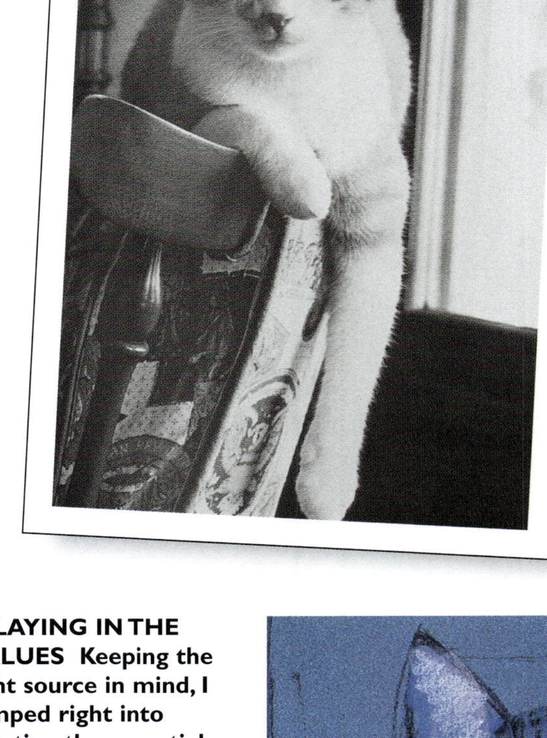

◄ **CHOOSING A REFERENCE** This photo contains enough information about value and shape to easily translate into color, especially since cat colors can be practically anything you want them to be!

► **BLOCKING IN THE SHAPES** Here are a few steps to show how I focus on shapes, values, and textures and the way they interrelate. As I sketched in the cat's general outline, I paid attention to where the different parts were in relation to one another. For example, the eyes are at the halfway point of the head and the nose is halfway between the eyes and the chin.

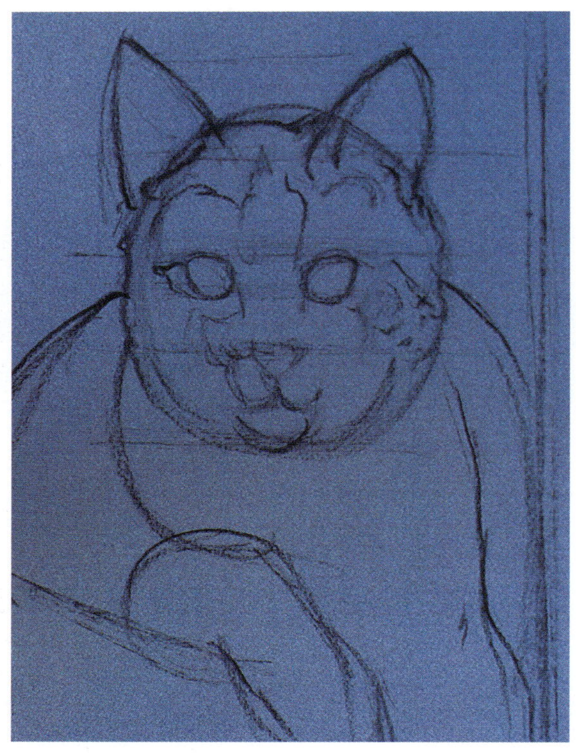

► **LAYING IN THE VALUES** Keeping the light source in mind, I jumped right into painting the essentials with hard pastels: light side, shadow side, yellow eyes, mouth, and nose. This helps me establish the drawing and value structure. I wasn't worried about detailing the fur texture yet, just with placing the varying values.

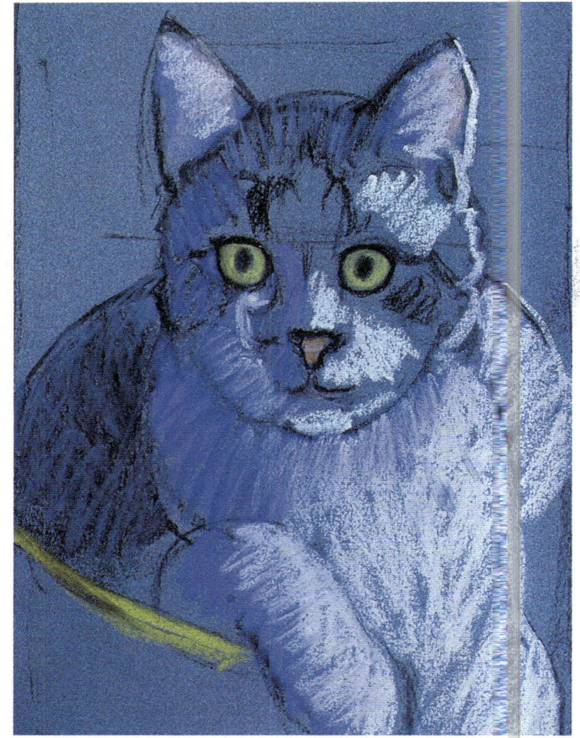

### Seeing Shape Relationships

I try to look at the wildlife subjects I paint as objectively as I can. Instead of thinking of them as specific animals, I think of them as a collection of light, medium, and dark shapes that fit together like pieces of a puzzle. When all the shapes are accurately copied and assembled, they become the animal I'm painting. This way I can get rid of any preconceptions I may have about what I *think* their shapes should look like and describe what shapes I really *see* instead.

► **TABBY CAT** After adding a background and blending and softening some areas with a stump, I applied strokes in the direction that the fur grows; refined the highlights and shadows; and detailed the eyes, nose, and whiskers. I left some of my pastel strokes visible, rather than blending them all, especially where I wanted to suggest long hair and whiskers.

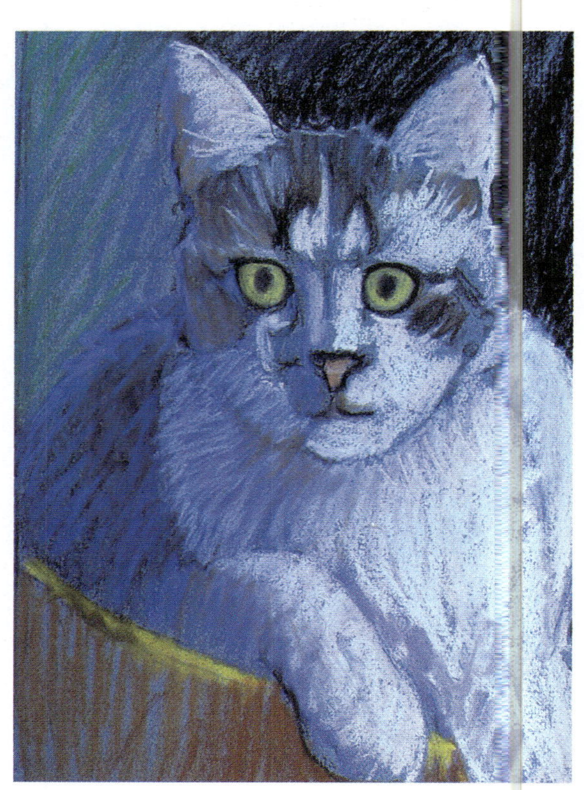

**Artist's Tip**

*As animals seldom stay still, it's easier to paint them from photos. The important thing when using photos is to improvise by changing the lighting and backgrounds, as I have done here.*

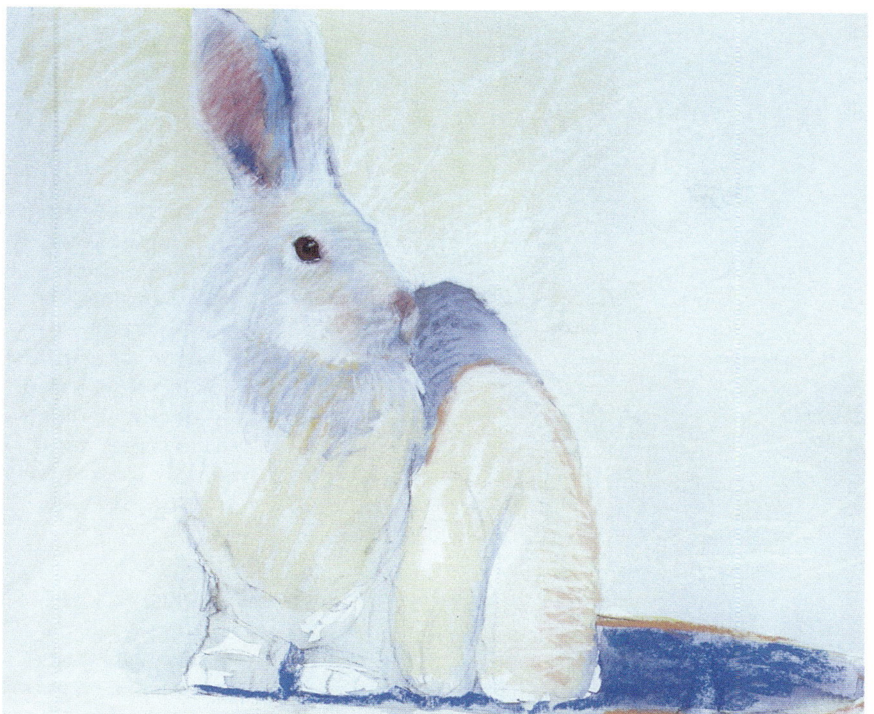

**SNOW RABBIT** I created the texture of this white rabbit's fur by slowly building up the grays, yellows, and blues, laying fine, light strokes over the dark areas. I let the chest area blend into the background to suggest very soft fur. But to keep the rabbit from becoming indistinguishable from its snowy surroundings, I left the shadow areas quite dark and made the edge along its back more defined than on its chest.

## Artist's Tip

*When painting animals, place strong lights and highlights on the side where the light is coming from. These are small, but important, details that really make the subject come to life.*

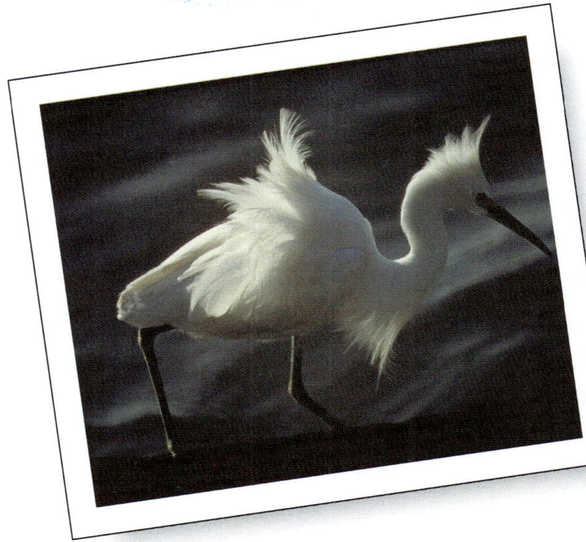

◄ **ALTERING YOUR REFERENCE PHOTO** This photo of a backlit egret is stunning but too poorly composed to be translated into a painting. Instead, I rearranged the composition and added lotus flowers to echo the shape of the bird's plumage.

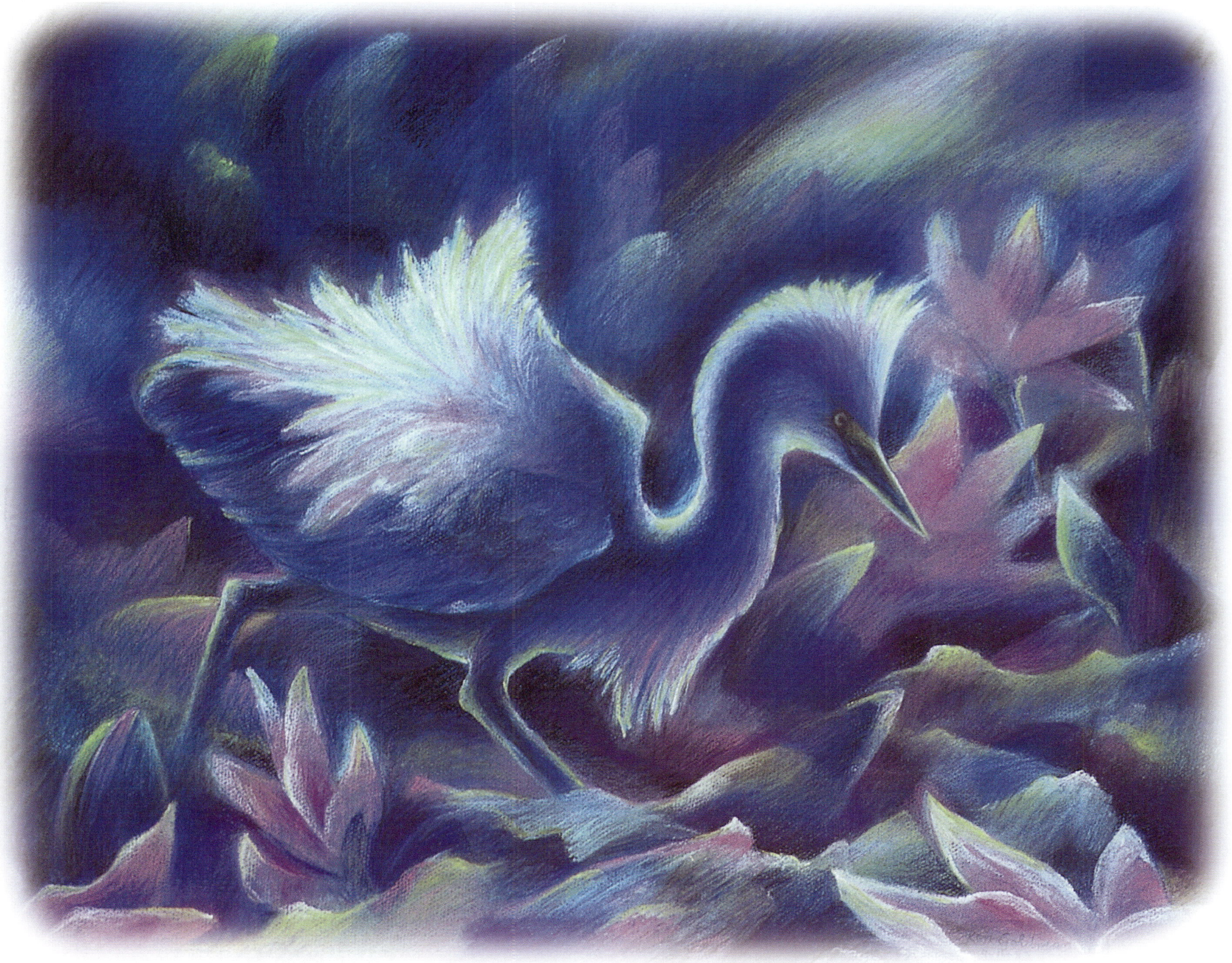

**LUMINOUS EGRET** This painting was done mostly with small, directional strokes. I created the glowing effect by placing darker values against the lights.

# Texturing Techniques

PASTEL IS A PERFECT MEDIUM for rendering textures, and rocks are a great way to practice painting them. They are also extremely common elements in landscapes, so you'll be glad you've learned to master them. By combining a few simple stroke techniques I demonstrate here, such as crosshatches, blending, and flat strokes, you'll be creating convincing textures in no time. Remember, as always, just start by simplifying the forms of your subject into basic shapes, such as cubes and spheres, and then get creative with textures!

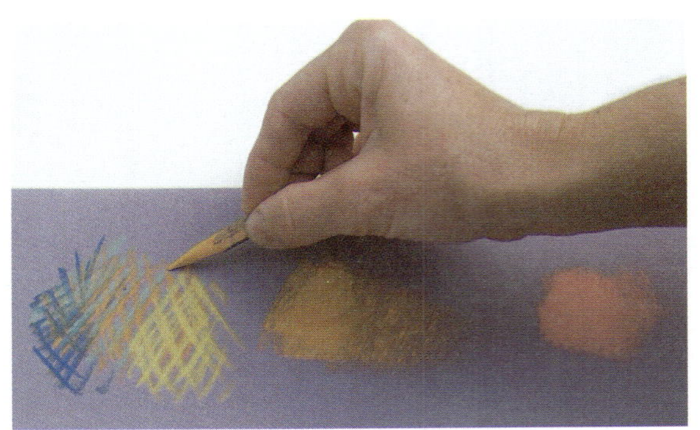

◄ **CROSSHATCHING** This is a great way to lay down colors without completely covering the underlying paper tone or base color. Simply overlapping strokes in different directions automatically creates an interesting texture.

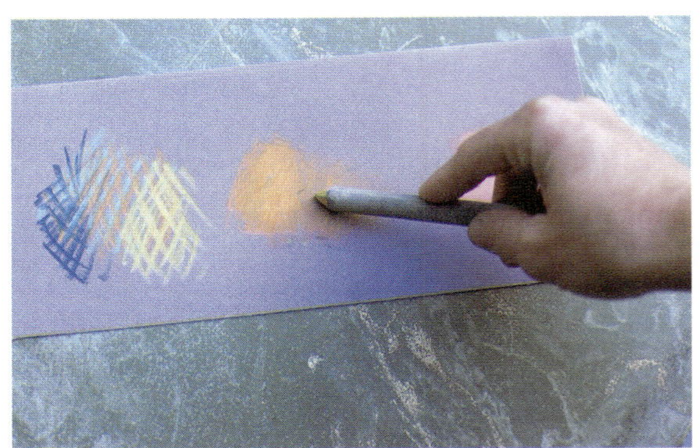

◄ **BLENDING** Using a stump or your finger, softly blend the crosshatched strokes together to create a smooth texture and subtle gradations of tone.

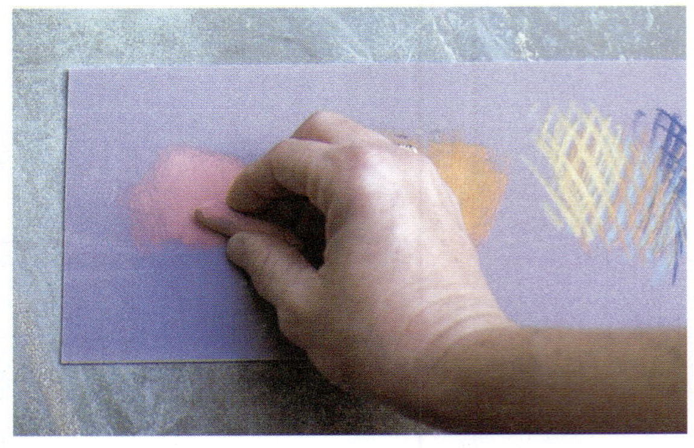

◄ **FLAT STROKES** Using the side of the pastel stick is a good way to cover large areas with color. Applied lightly, it can be used to glaze a new color over an existing one. To glaze, very lightly stroke one color on top of another color.

### Applying Texture Techniques to Rocks

I use a combination of strokes to create the texture of rocks, as you can see in the boulder below. I use crosshatched strokes to imitate the roughness of a rock's surface, which is especially appropriate for granite. Blended strokes are suitable for smooth, river rocks or for indistinct shadow areas of rougher stones. I also use flat strokes for any kind of rock, mainly to unify the other strokes and incorporate all the colors.

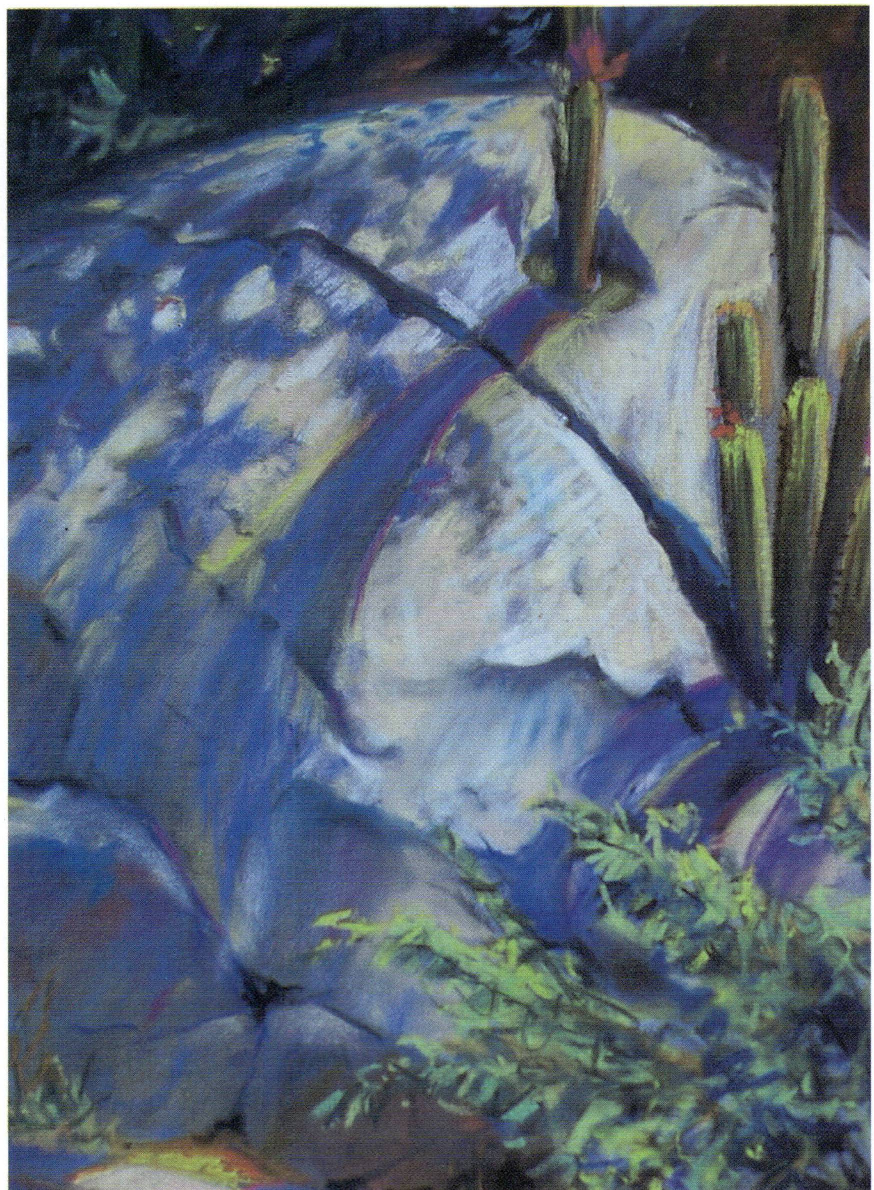

**CACTUS BOULDER** I began my drawing by visualizing this boulder as an imperfect sphere and viewing the cacti as cylinders. I applied grays and yellows with crosshatching and blending, adding blue shadows to help delineate the overall form. I created the yellow tinges with soft, flat strokes at the end. Notice that I used contrasting textures in the subjects and the background, which also help make this boulder really stand out.

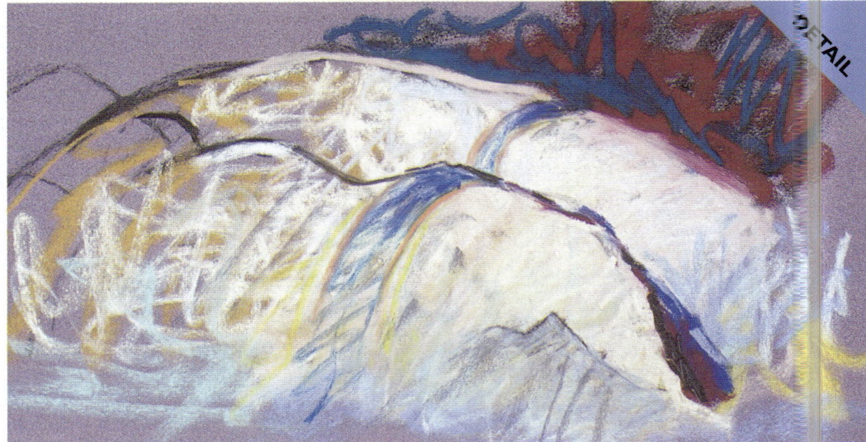


**COMBINING TECHNIQUES** This drawing shows one of the early steps of the final painting of the boulder shown at left. Here I used the three different textures to begin building up the form, with mostly crosshatching and flat strokes on the left, and blending on the right.

### Contrasting Textures of Rocks and Water

Rocks are often simply one element in a landscape, but I will paint a solitary rock if its form and texture appeal to me. In fact, I am particularly fascinated by the contrast of the solid, static form of rocks against the fluidity of moving water, and I find many examples at the ocean. The dramatic tension between the stationary rock and the fluid sea is the focus of the pastel painting at right.

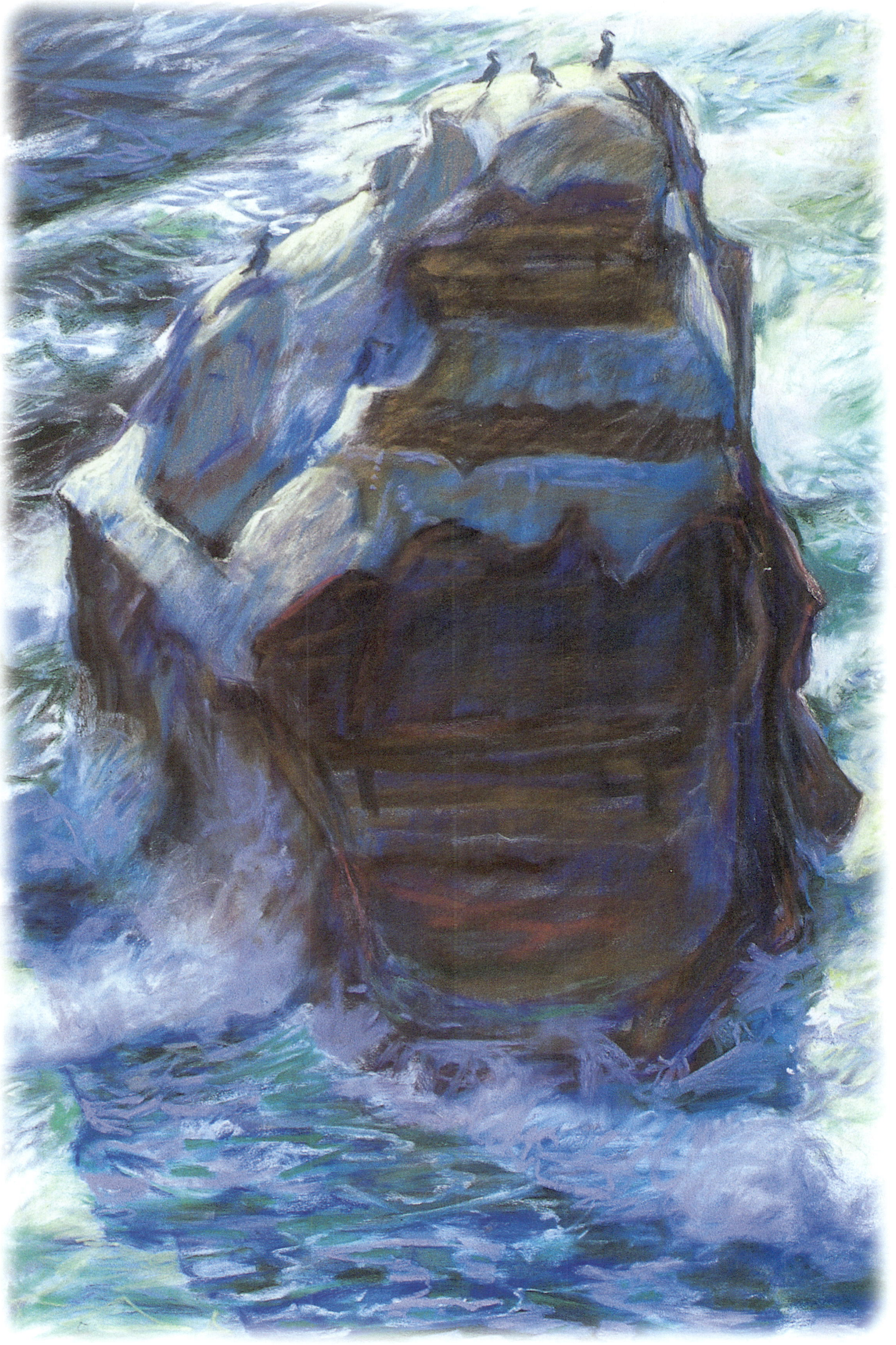

**◄ CORMORANT ROCK** In this painting of a rock protruding from the ocean, I developed the form and texture of the dark rock using flat strokes of yellow ochre, deep magenta, and blue in the shadow and subtle flat strokes of red and yellow on the light guano. Here I applied many layers of pastel and left only a little of the paper tone showing through, which adds to the feeling of solidity I wanted to convey. For the water, I used a variety of greens, blues, and yellows with white, and I kept the tones light to contrast with the rock. I also let the paper show through a bit under the water, which gives it a less solid feeling compared to the rock.

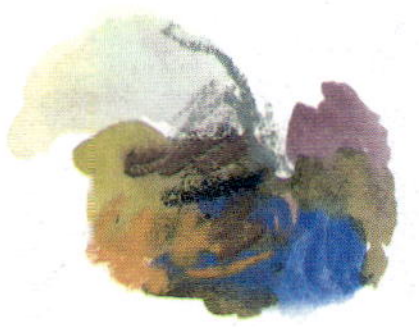

*Rock and guano: White, yellow ochre, light red, deep magenta, raw sienna, and blue*

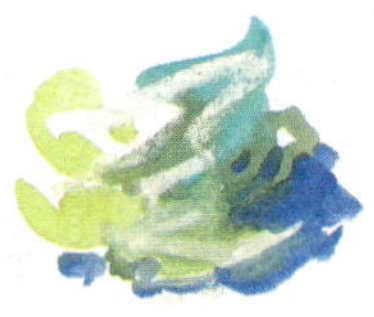

*Water: Various greens, blues, yellows, and white*

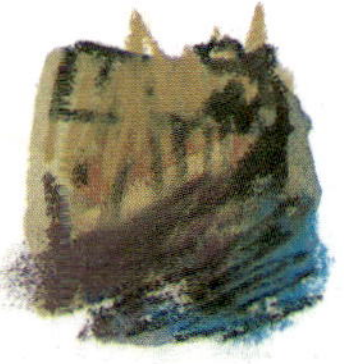

*Textures: Overlays of deep magenta, red, blue, and black*

# Blending Pastels

ALTHOUGH YOU CAN MIX PASTEL colors, the more colors you have to start with, the easier it is to get all the colors you want by blending them together. The pastel sets I've recommended—including hard, soft, pencils, and grays—will give you ample colors to mix what you need by overlapping strokes and blending the pastels on the paper. The charts on this page explain a few terms and show you how to combine primary colors to create secondary ones and how to tint, tone, and shade.

## Creating Values

A good pastel set has at least three values of each color and at least three values of gray. To expand my range of values, I add neutrals to my colors, mixing them together directly on the painting surface. I add white to *tint* a color (making it lighter in value), I add gray to *tone* a color (creating a medium value), and I add black to *shade* a color (achieving a dark value). The chart below shows what results you get when you mix different colors: you can tint or shade a primary color or mix two primaries to create a secondary color. Adding white, gray, and black to the secondaries gives you the wide array of tints, tones, and shades found in your pastel set.

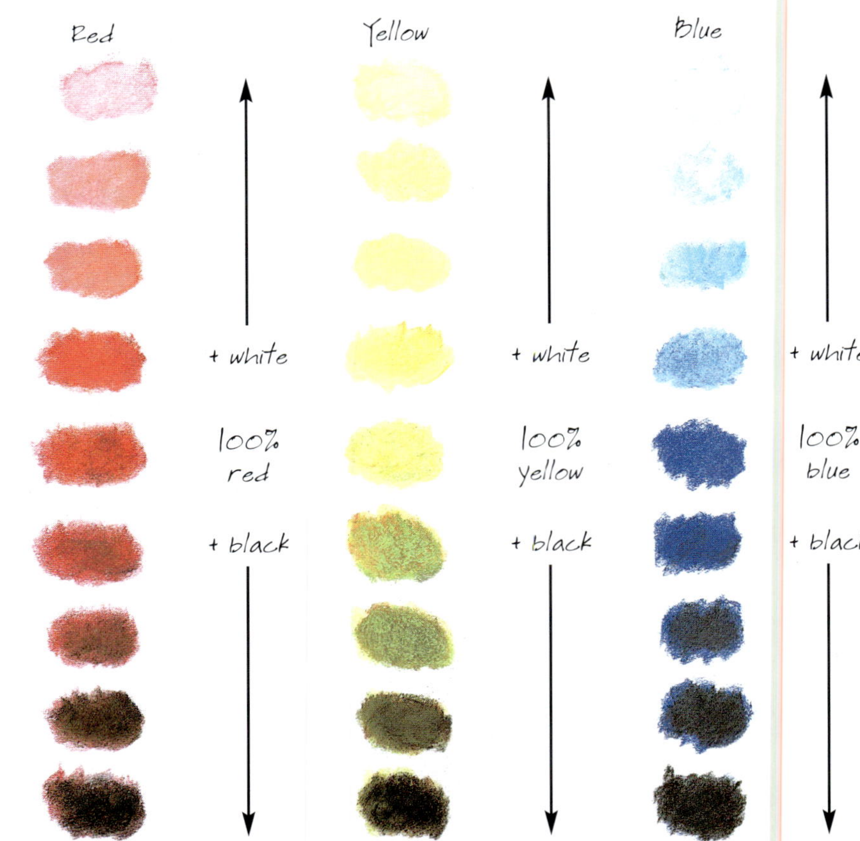


**MAKING A VALUE SCALE** The chart above is a simple value scale for each of the three primary colors, showing the range of values from almost white to almost black. To make a value chart, start with the pure primary in the center. Create the tints above by adding progressively more and more white to the pigment, and produce the shades below by gradually increasing the amount of black added.

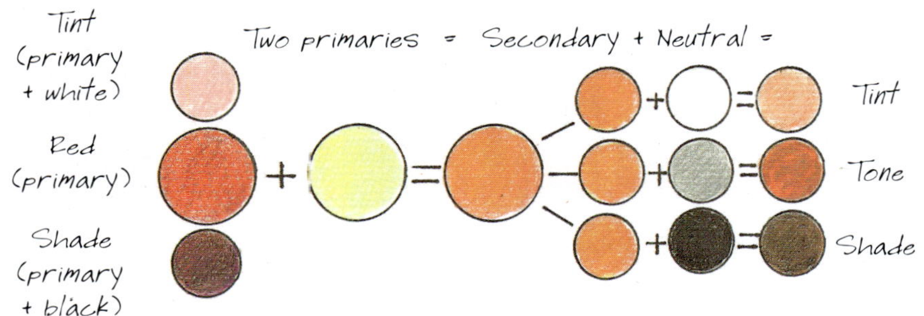


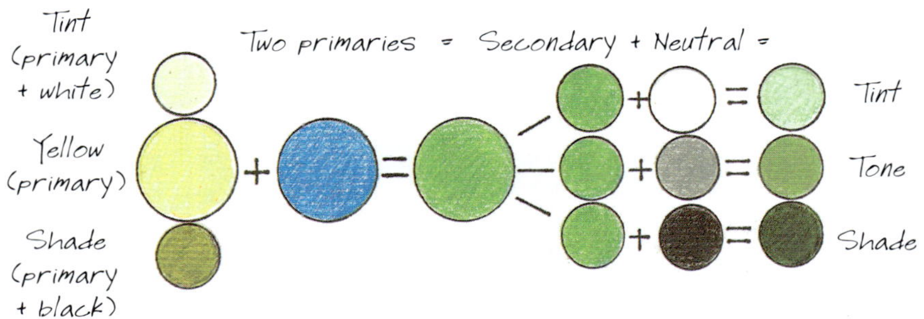


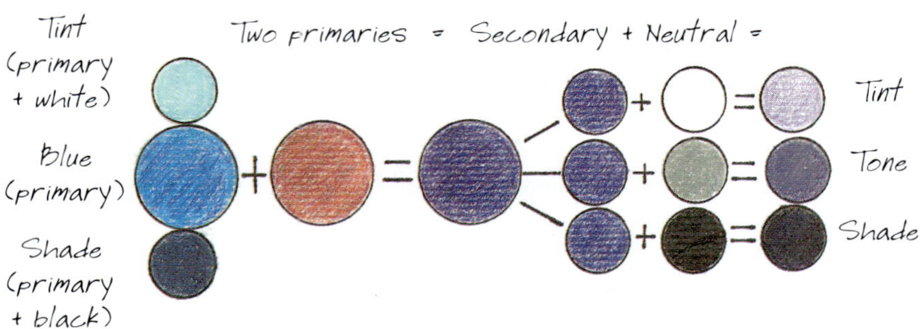


**MIXING PASTELS** The circles on the left represent the primary colors (red, yellow, and blue) with their tints and shades (white or black added) above and below. The middle circles show how mixing two primaries creates a secondary. The circles on the right show what the secondaries look like when tinted with white, toned with gray, or shaded with black.

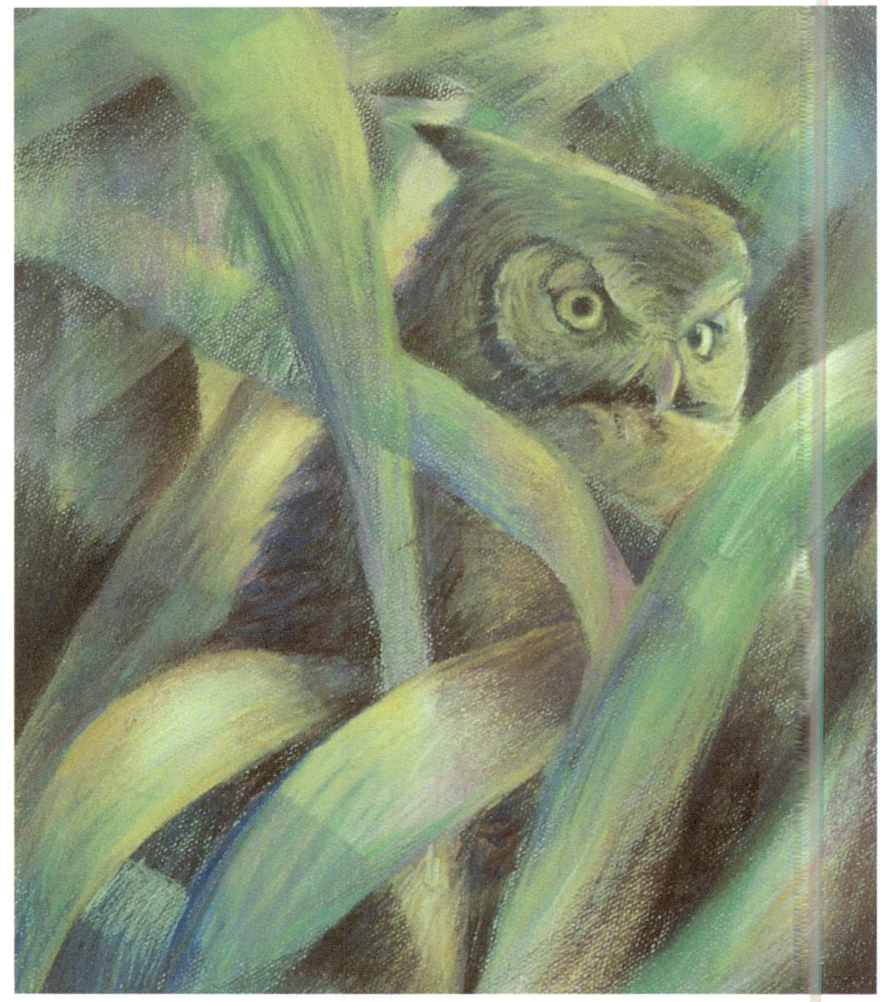

**TONAL OWL** This painting of an owl shows how soft and subtle the colors become when toned with varying values of gray. In fact, you could say the general color scheme of this painting is gray. Even the accent colors of yellow and blue have been softly muted with gray, keeping the overall feeling of the painting quiet and still.

► **SPRING FLOWERS**
**This field is a great example of how complementary colors create vibrancy and excitement. My overall color scheme is orange and red, but I added green—the complement of red—as an accent color. To see just how complements react, cover the green with your hand and notice how much less potent the red seems without it.**

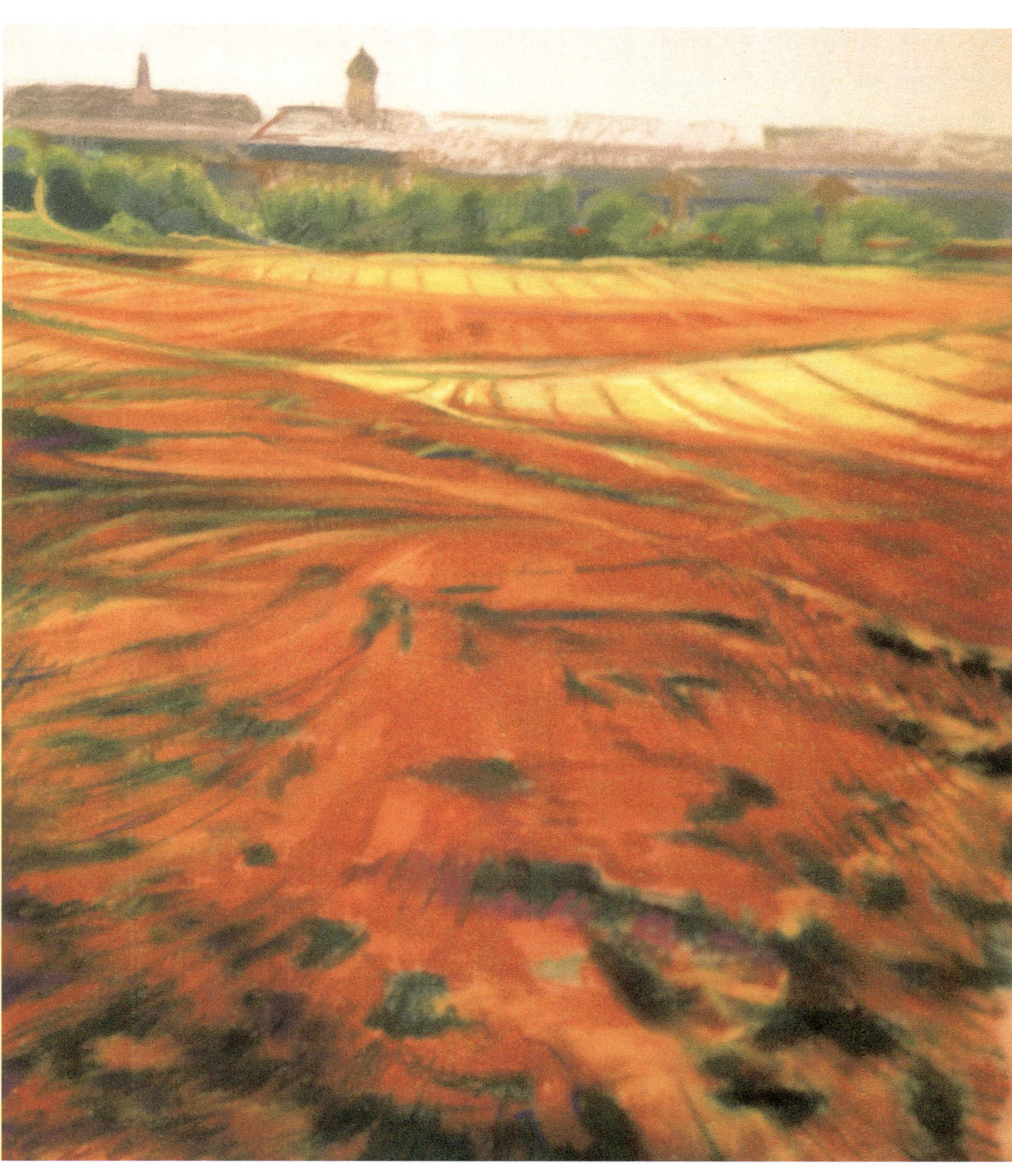

### Choosing a Color Scheme

When deciding on a color scheme for a painting, I think about values, shades, and tones, knowing that more intense or pure colors are more exciting and that toned colors are more soothing. Also, certain colors, called *complements* or *complementary opposites* (they are opposite one another on the color wheel), add an extra sense of vibrancy when they are placed near one another. (You're probably all familiar with the color wheel and complementary colors, but if you want to learn more, see William F. Powell's *Color and How to Use It* in Walter Foster's Artist's Library series.) The values I choose, the level of intensity I employ, and where I place my colors will all depend on the feeling I want to convey in my painting.

◄ **FOGGY MEADOW**
**In this painting, the colors are primarily blue and purple, with yellow (the complement of purple) as an accent color. Again, cover the yellow with your hand and notice how much the impact is lessened. Keep this in mind as you paint, and try pairing complements when you want a little oomph!**

Cadmium yellow and cadmium red light

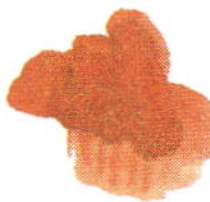

Deep red

Magenta, cadmium red, and dark green

Light blue, yellow, orange, and light gray

Black and dark blue

Dark blue and turquoise

**Artist's Tip**

Just as black is used to darken pastels in the factory, you can use it to deepen your own colors. A good way to make certain areas darker and richer is to add black first and then go over it again with a pure color.

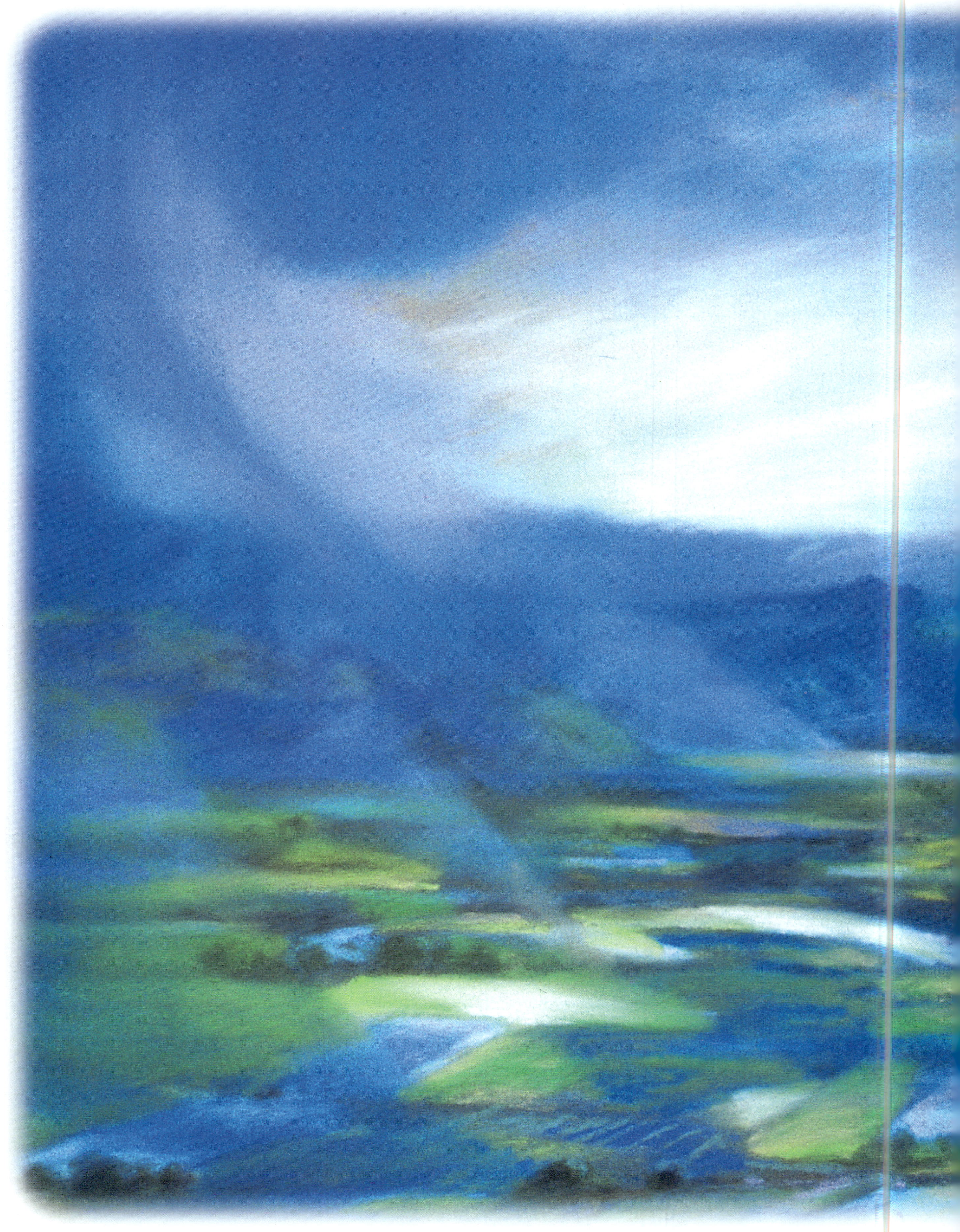

**EXPRESSING MOOD** In this painting, I used the veils of rain as a way to add interest, movement, and mood. Unlike a cloudscape at high altitudes, a sea-level la

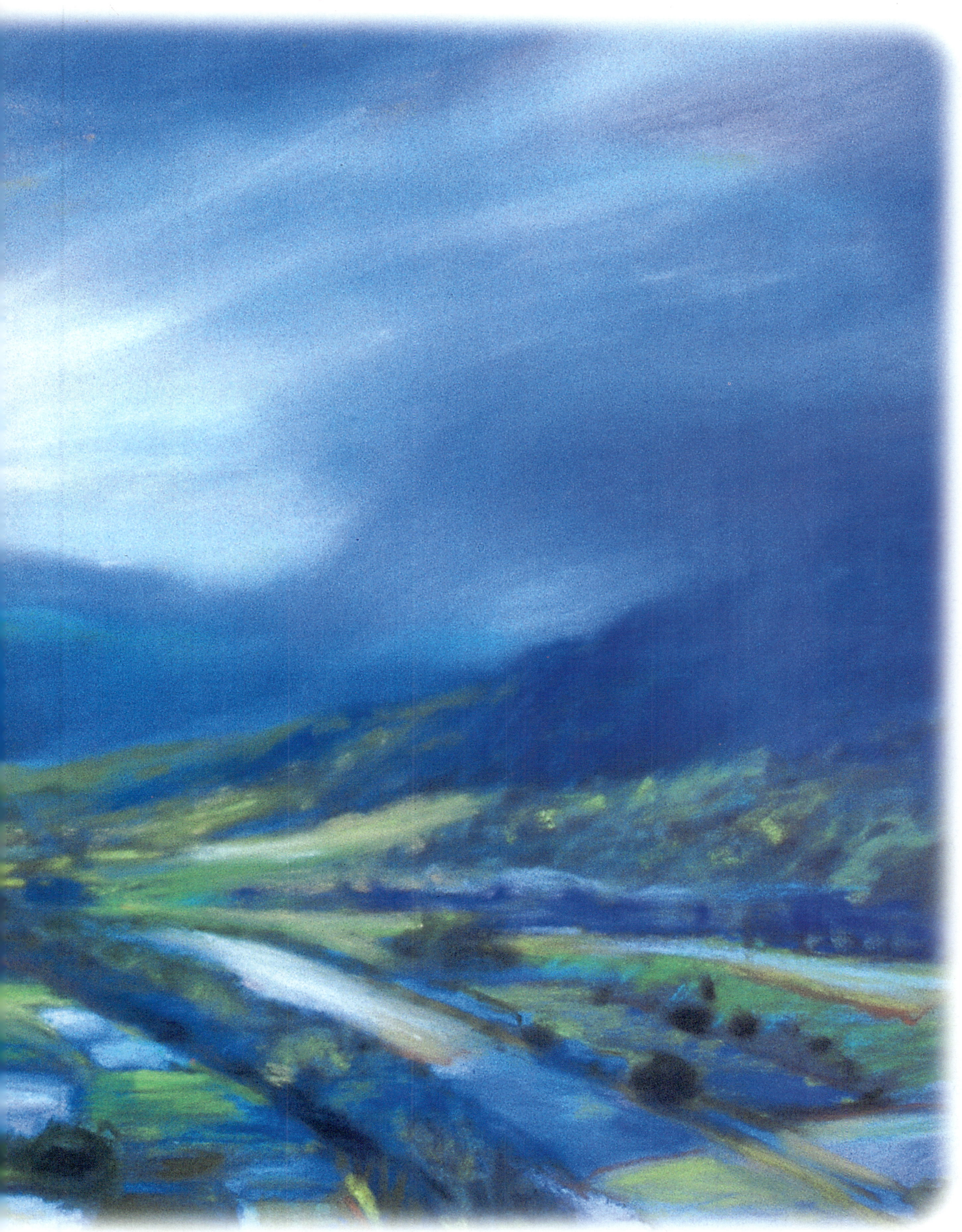

ıas softer edges. Although I began this picture on location, I changed the scene so it ended up as a partly imaginary landscape.

# Capturing a Time of Day

DID YOU KNOW THAT the *color* of light and shadows is affected by the angle of the sun? This is because our atmosphere is much thicker at the horizon than it is higher up, and its density affects the colors we see. Like most landscape painters, I prefer to work during late afternoon—"the golden hour"—because colors keep getting warmer and richer while the lush blue shadows grow longer. At dawn, colors are as rich as at dusk, but they quickly fade as the sun rises. At midday, colors aren't vibrant and shadows appear darker.

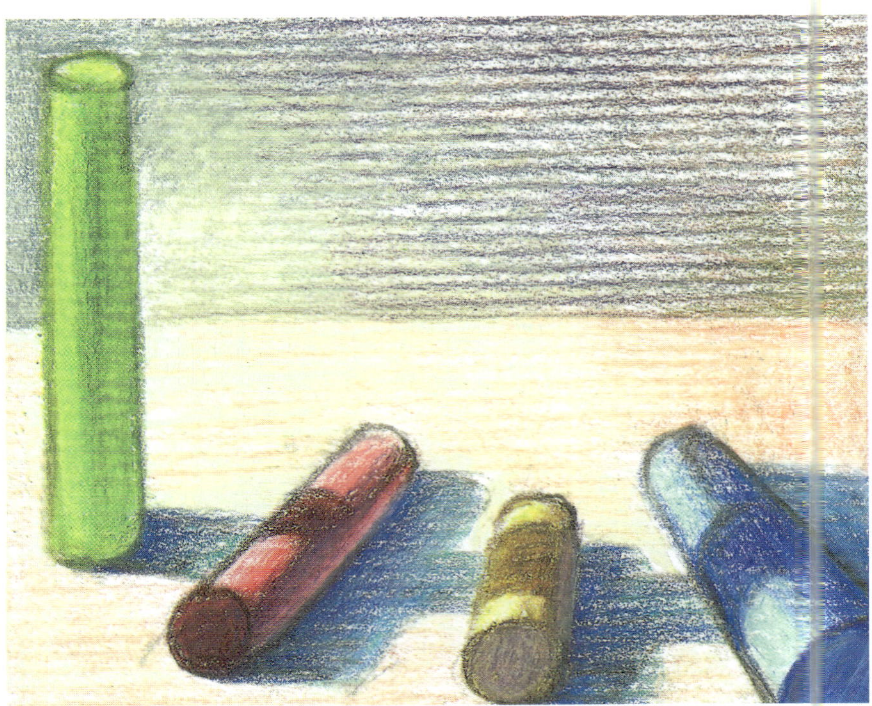

**CHANGING SHADOWS** This shows how a shadow changes color. It shifts from blue-violet on the paper to red-violet on the red stick, yellow-violet on the yellow stick, and deep blue-violet on the blue stick.

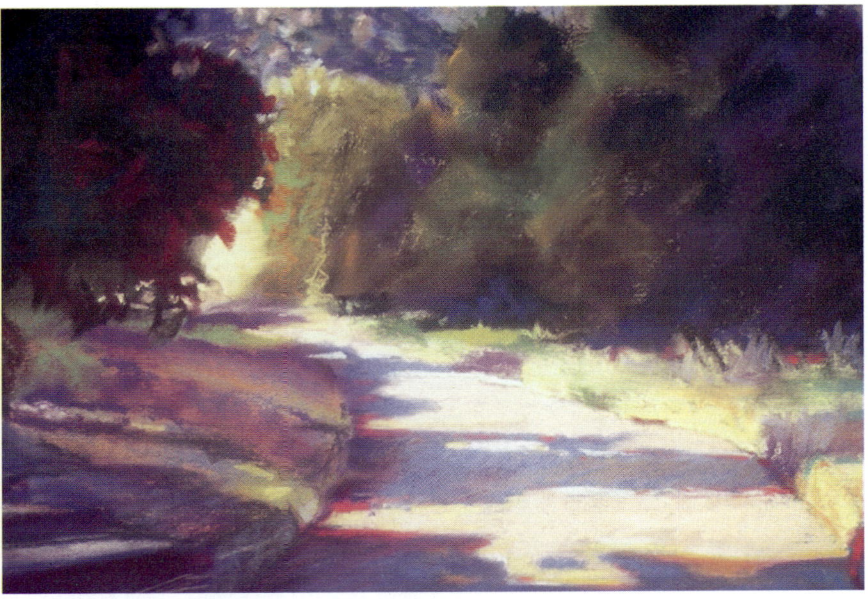

**EARLY MORNING SHADOWS** I especially like to paint cast shadows over curbs, grasses, shrubs, and uneven ground. For this kind of terrain, I make the shadows climb and drop to follow the form. Here the blue-violet shadows are warmed by the ochres of the dusty pathway and the reddish transition areas along the edges of the shadows.

### Determining the Color of Shadows

Shadows are a mix of many different colors. They are made partly of the complementary opposite of the light source, so if the lighting is yellow, for example, the shadow will contain some violet—the complement of yellow. Shadows also take on some of the color of the objects they fall on, so a violet shadow on a blue object will be made of violet and a little blue. This means that when a shadow is progressively cast over a number of objects or parts of a landscape, it constantly changes color and value (lightness or darkness), depending on the color and value of what it falls upon. The three paintings on these pages illustrate the concepts of time of day and the changing values and colors in shadows.

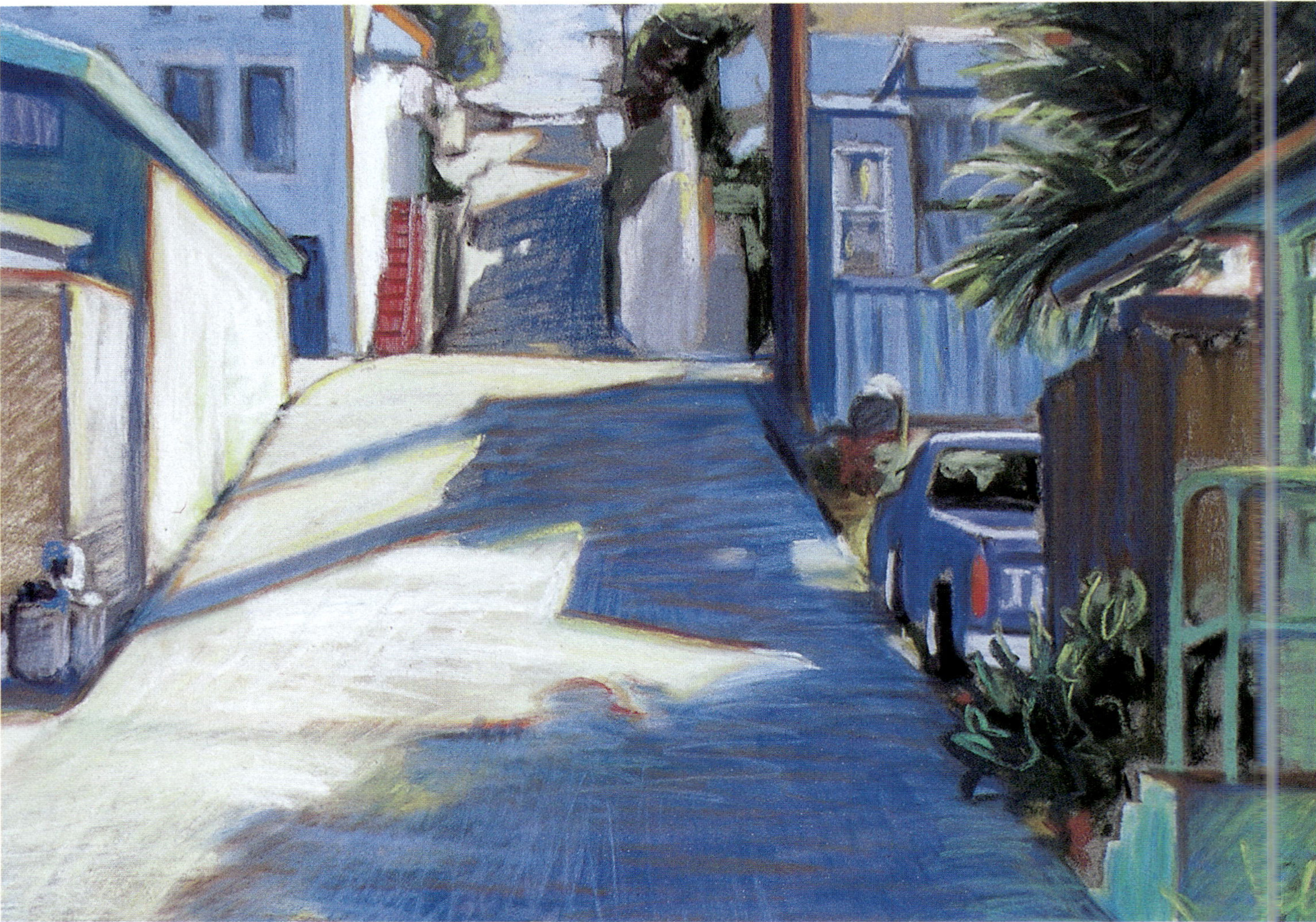

▸ **AFTERNOON SHADOWS** I am influenced by the streetscapes of artist Wayne Thiebaud, except I find that alleys are not as busy to paint in! Notice how much lighter and grayer the farthest shadow is, and how the shadow shapes are used as a design element for this composition. Because concrete is almost white, the colors of the alley don't greatly affect the shadow colors.

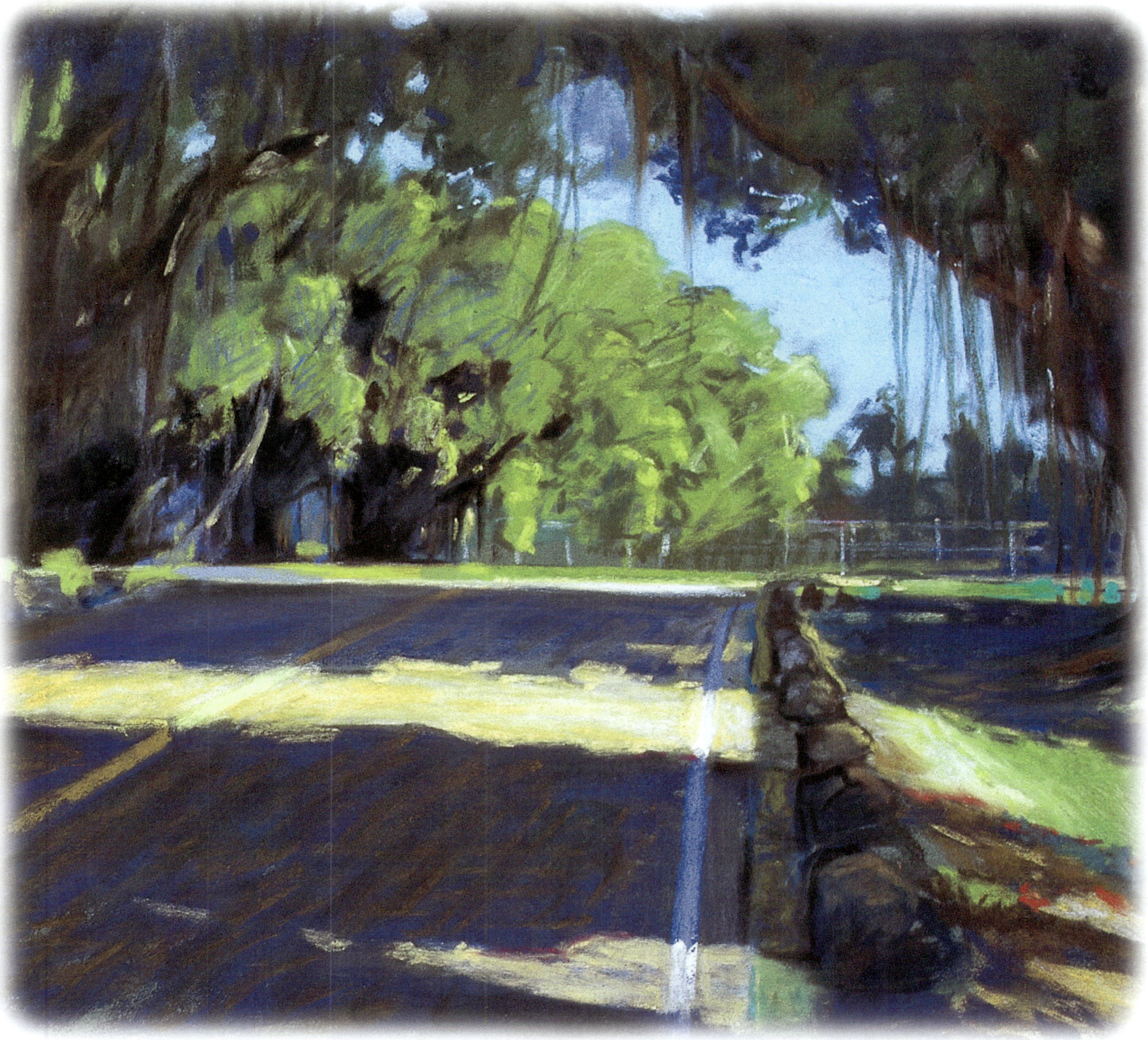

**MIDDAY SHADOWS** At noon, shadows are very hard and sharp, but they still have color. Here the lines become raw sienna and blue where the shadows fall.

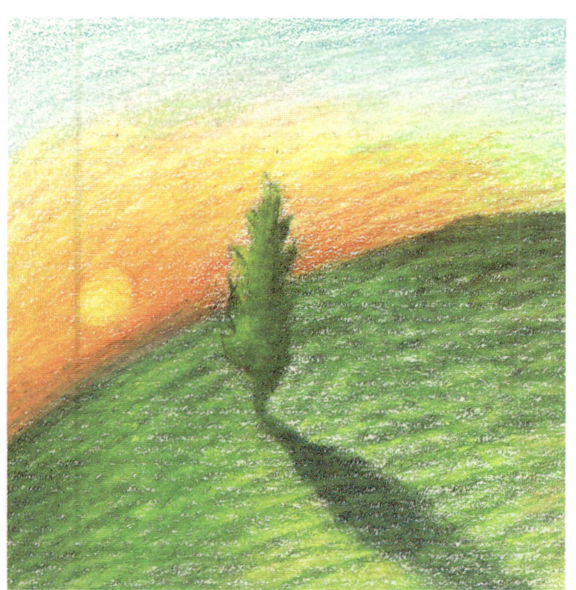

**DAWN** On a clear morning, the sun rises in yellows and oranges. The air has cooled overnight, and moisture has settled the day's dust. Through this cleaner air, we see less red and more yellow.

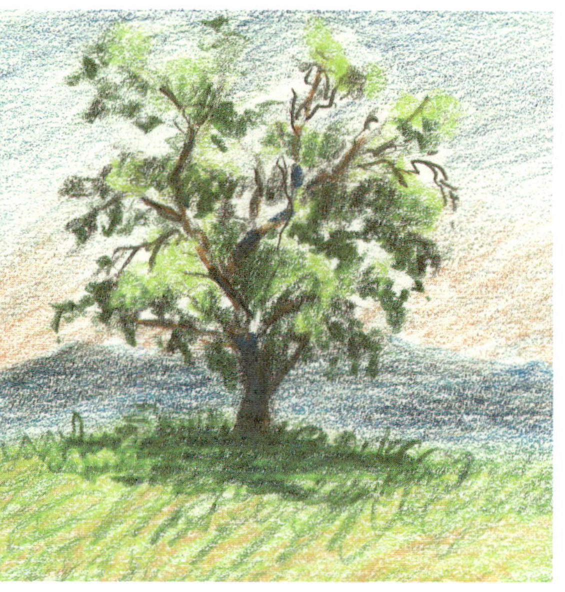

**MIDDAY** At noon, dust has been stirred up, making the atmosphere more dense than in the morning. At this time of day, colors look faded, and shadows are darker and more intense.

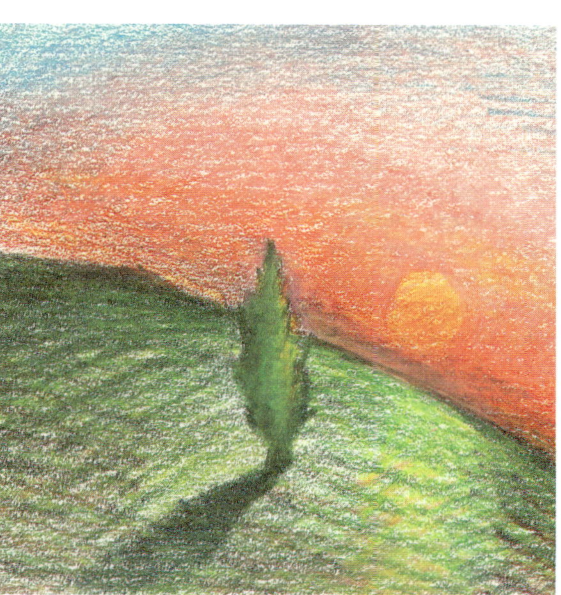

**DUSK** After a bustling day of city life, dust has built up in the atmosphere, so it has become very dense. For that reason, sunsets are often redder or pinker than sunrises.

# Rendering Puffy Clouds

CLOUDS CAN BE DRAMATIC and thick, soft and billowy, or light and wispy. Clouds are generally what gives skyscapes their drama and interest, and sunsets their glorious colors. I love using pastels for painting clouds because I can make cottony soft blends and create translucent effects, especially with my set of soft sticks. And with the range of vibrant colors available, I can even attempt to interpret the brilliant colors of the rising and setting sun that reflect on the clouds' surface.

## Giving Clouds Form

Beginners often paint clouds as if they were a solid mass of cotton, when in reality clouds have distinct tops, sides, and bottoms. They have a form, just as any other object does, that needs to be rendered with varying values. If you keep this in mind, you will be able to draw and paint believable clouds. Copy the examples shown here for practice.

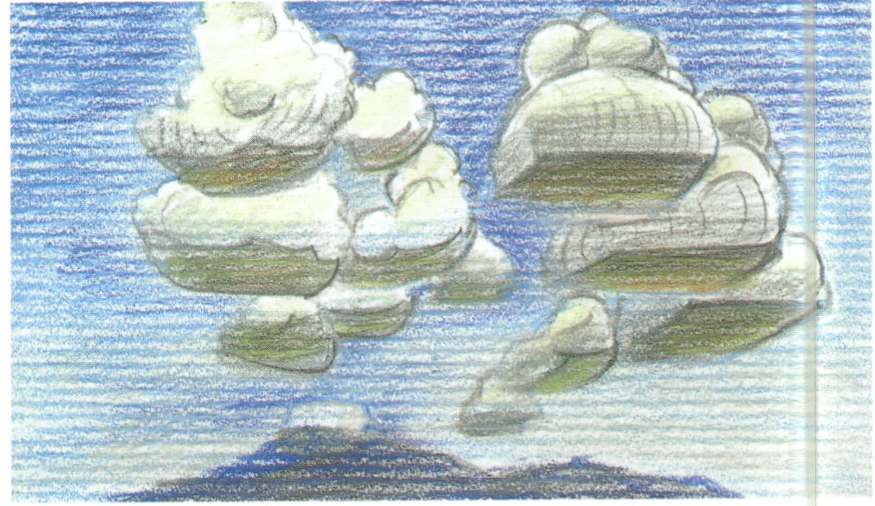

**SEEING THE FORMS** In this sketch, the light source is coming from above the clouds. Here I made the clouds seem to recede into the distance by narrowing their shapes the farther away they get.

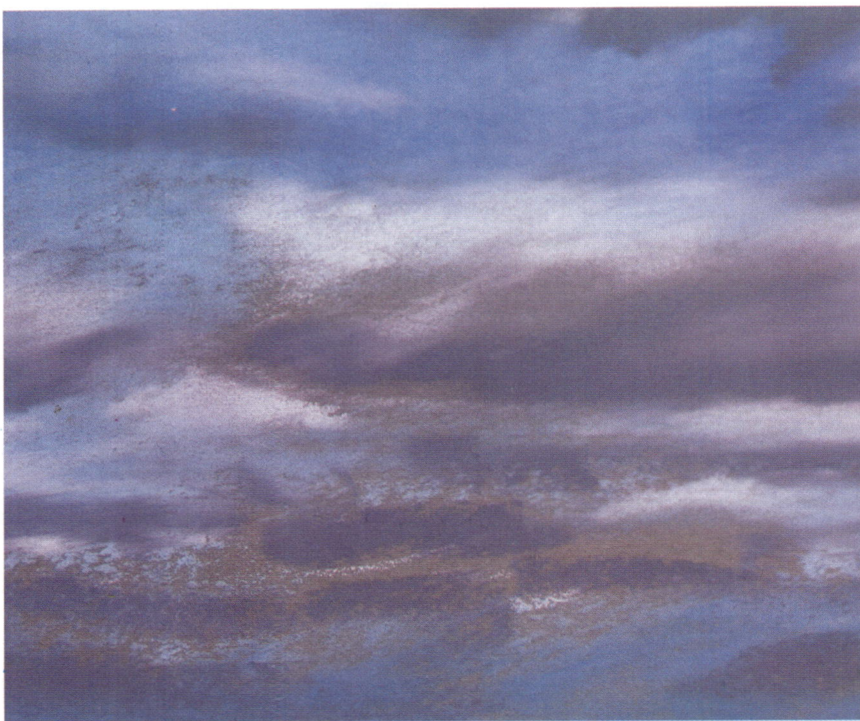

**◄ PAINTING CLOUDS** On a middle-toned paper, I laid down the bottom of the clouds first with gray and indigo. I let a little paper show through for the sides, then added white for the top and blended a little. I used the blue sky and gray from the secondary clouds to define the top of the largest clouds. Whenever I want to show a brilliant white, I add a little orange or pink. This eliminates the pastiness of pure white.

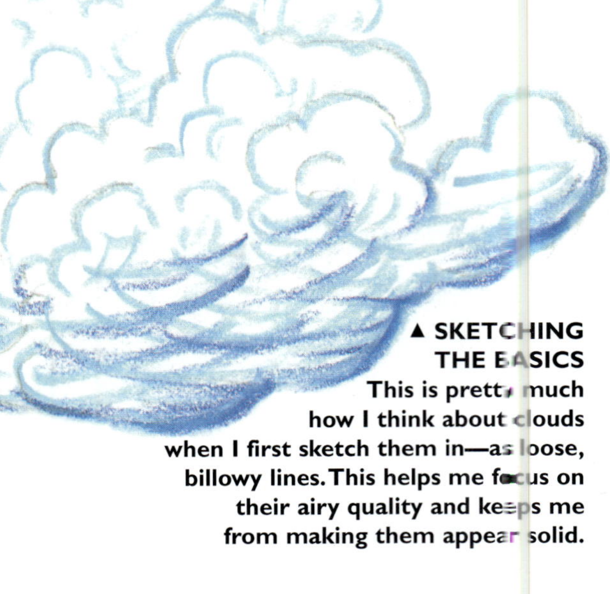

**▲ SKETCHING THE BASICS** This is pretty much how I think about clouds when I first sketch them in—as loose, billowy lines. This helps me focus on their airy quality and keeps me from making them appear solid.

**► DEPICTING CLOUDS FROM ABOVE** This is the way cumulus clouds look at 14,000 feet of hand-numbing tropical altitude! With my soft pastels and blending strokes, I established the general forms of the clouds, using more white for the distant clouds and letting some of the color of the volcanic earth beneath the clouds show through. The air is very clear at this altitude, so I added some sharper details in the mountain with my pastel pencils.

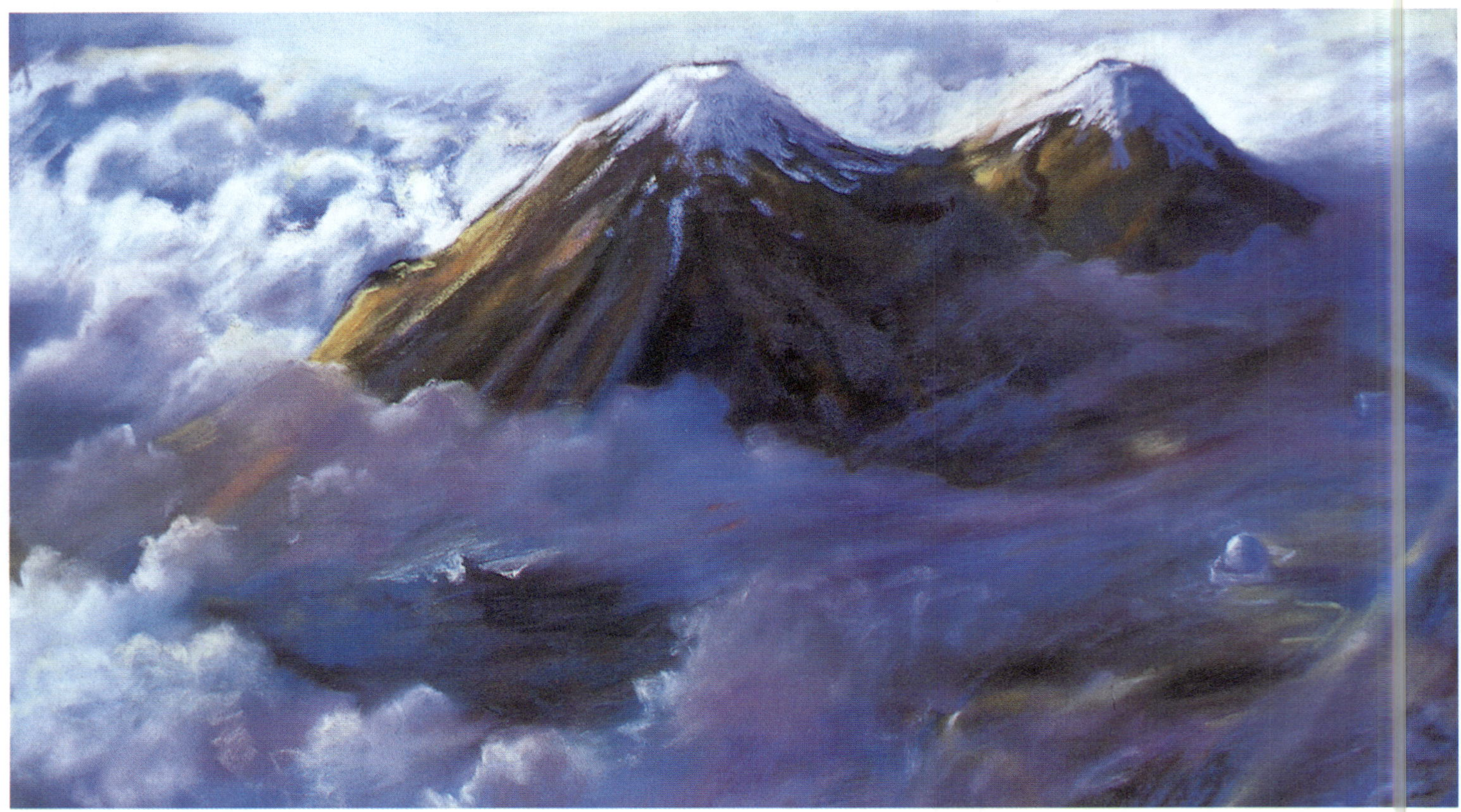

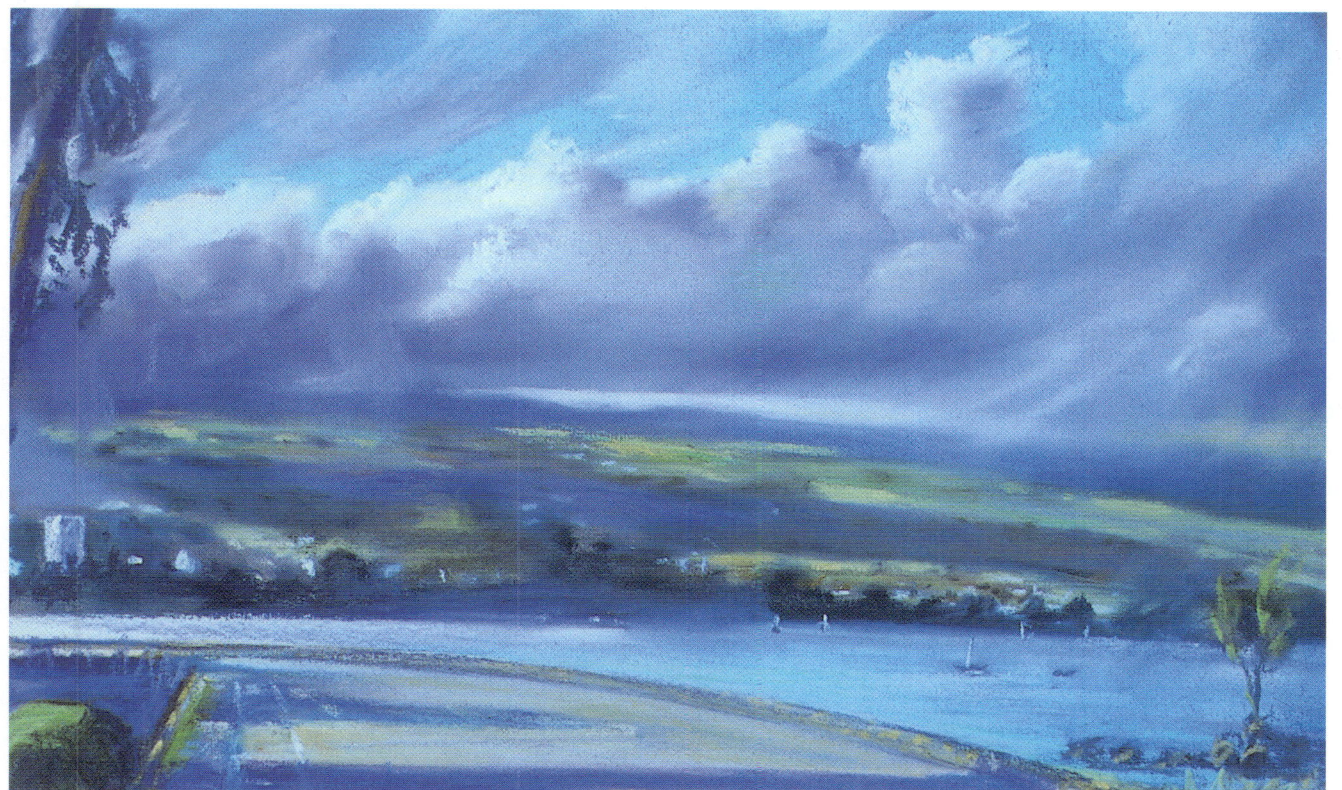

**◂ SHOWING CLOUDS FROM AFAR** I always make sure the lighting stays consistent throughout my composition. Here the sun is rather high in the sky, and the light is coming from the left. Therefore, I placed the lights on the boulders and bushes on the left side, and made the shadows fall to the right and slightly front. I thought about the mountain and the sky the same way, making sure they appeared to be lit by a light source coming from the left. I painted the shadows on the distant clouds with flat strokes of blue and gray, mingled into the flat strokes of white and light orange.

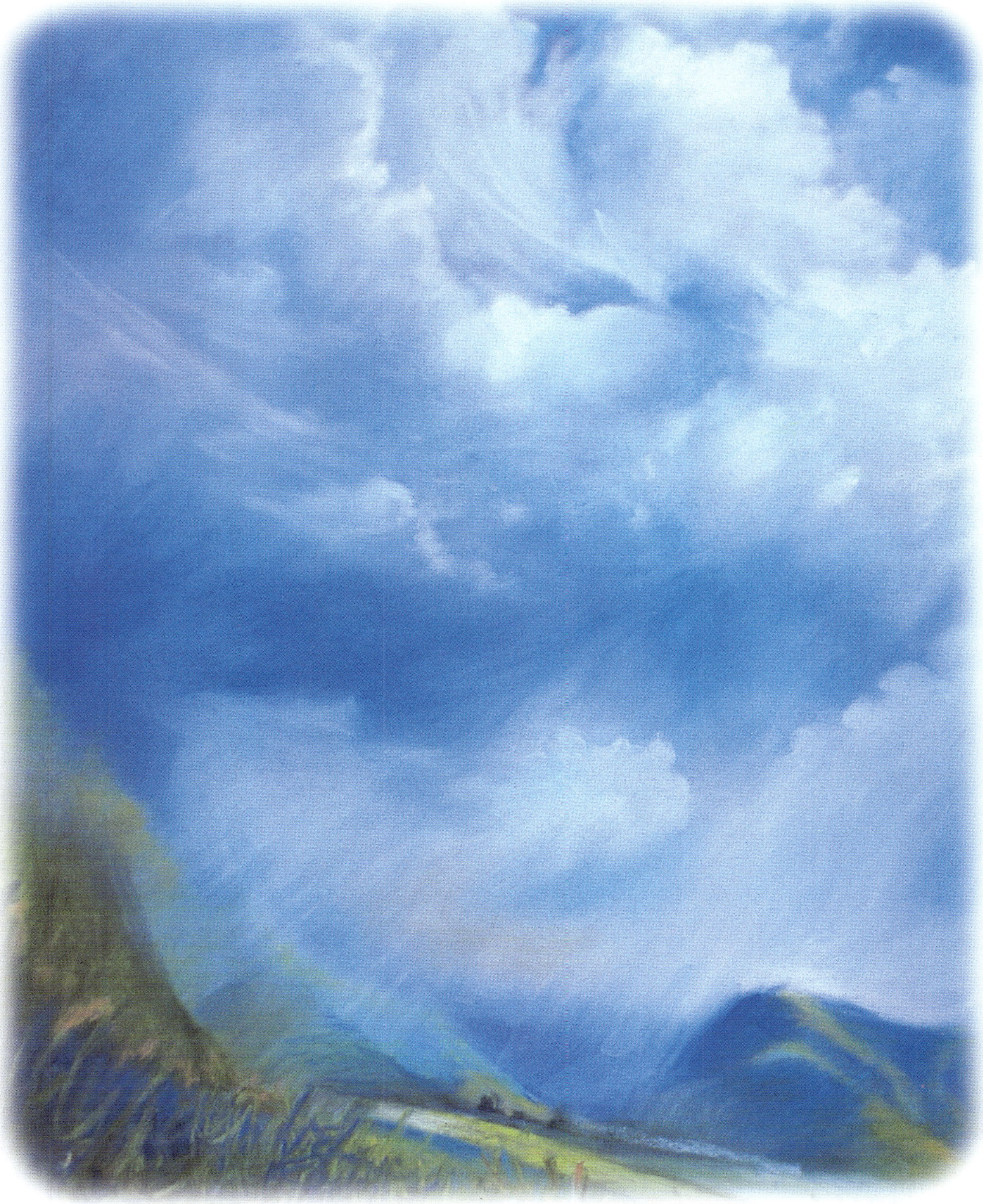

**◂ ADDING DRAMA** Rain clouds can be very dramatic and awe-inspiring, so I focused all the attention in this painting on the sky, using dark, muted tones, large forms, and blended strokes to suggest a brewing storm. To contrast with the softly blended sky, I added texture in the foreground grass using short strokes with the side of my pastels.

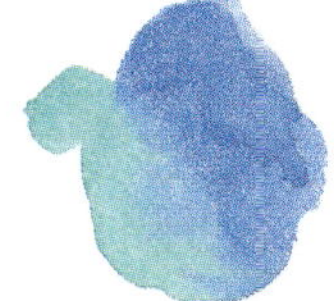

Light sky values: Cobalt blue and green

Medium sky values: Cobalt blue and cadmium orange

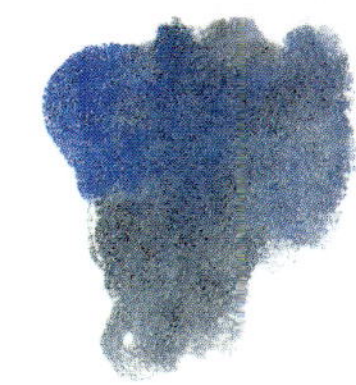

Dark sky values: Dark blue and dark gray

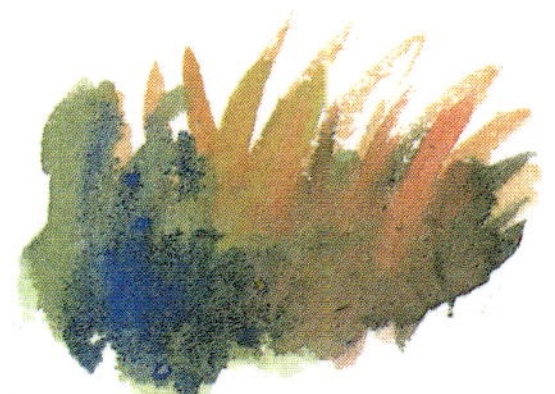

Grass: Yellow ochre, blue, and cadmium orange

# Portraying Flowers

ALMOST EVERY ARTIST I KNOW has painted flowers, probably because they are so varied in color, size, and shape that there always seems to be something new to discover and depict. Some flowers are mysterious, some are soothing, and some explode with excitement and drama. With its rich and brilliant colors, pastel is the perfect medium for capturing the varied colors and textures of flowers, whether as part of a still life, as part of a garden, or as a full-frame composition.

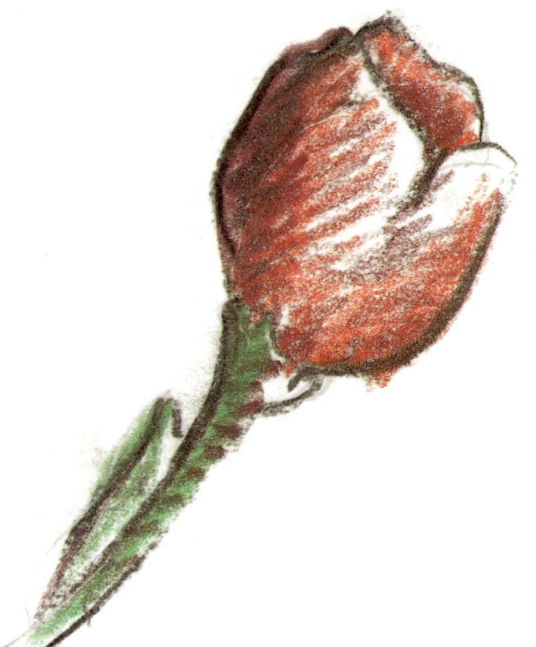

**◄ BLOCKING IN Whether I'm painting a single blossom or a whole bouquet, I begin by simplifying the overall shape of my flower subject. Here I started with my hard pastels and freely blocked in the extremes of light and dark. I used overlapping strokes in different directions to blend the colors, rather than using my fingers, so as not to muddy the colors.**

**► DEVELOPING THE FORMS I began this vase of flowers with hard pastels, just as I did with the single flower above. Then I used my soft pastels to add shadows to the flowers and to make the vase look three-dimensional. To give the vase depth, I concentrated on the light at the top of the vase and darkened it toward the bottom, letting the red bands nearly vanish into the shadows.**

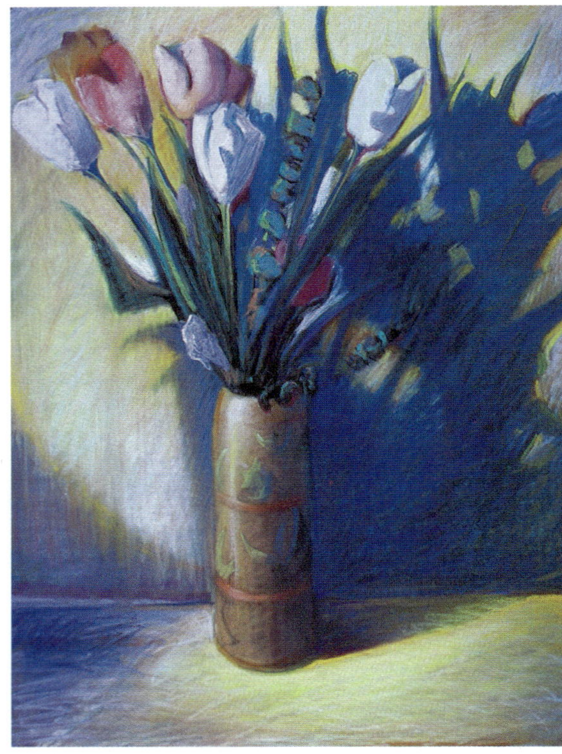

### Painting Flowers in Pastel

If you are just beginning to paint in pastel, flowers are the perfect place to start. For one thing, unless you are doing a botanical illustration, you don't need to worry about creating an exact likeness. And with just a few simple strokes, you can paint convincing blossoms in no time. For almost any flower, I use flat strokes for the petals and leaves, and a chiseled edge for the veins and details. I build up the color in layers and vary the pressure I use, bearing down on the light accents and lightly glazing the dark sides with a soft, flat stroke of a deeper shade of the same color, as shown in the tulips above.

## Painting a Base with Watercolor

To save my pastels and to add variety to the look of my paintings, I sometimes tone the paper first with watercolor. Then I apply pastels over the wash to indicate seeds, textures, accents, and even subtly blended tones, letting a lot of the watercolor base show through.

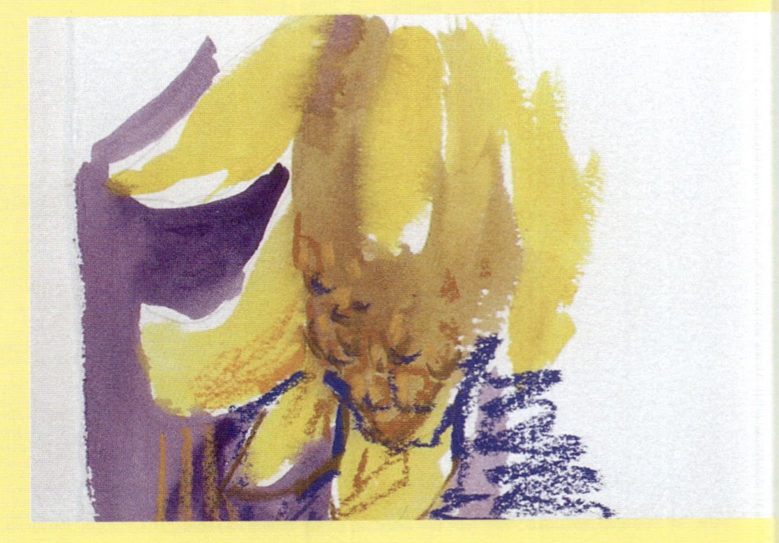

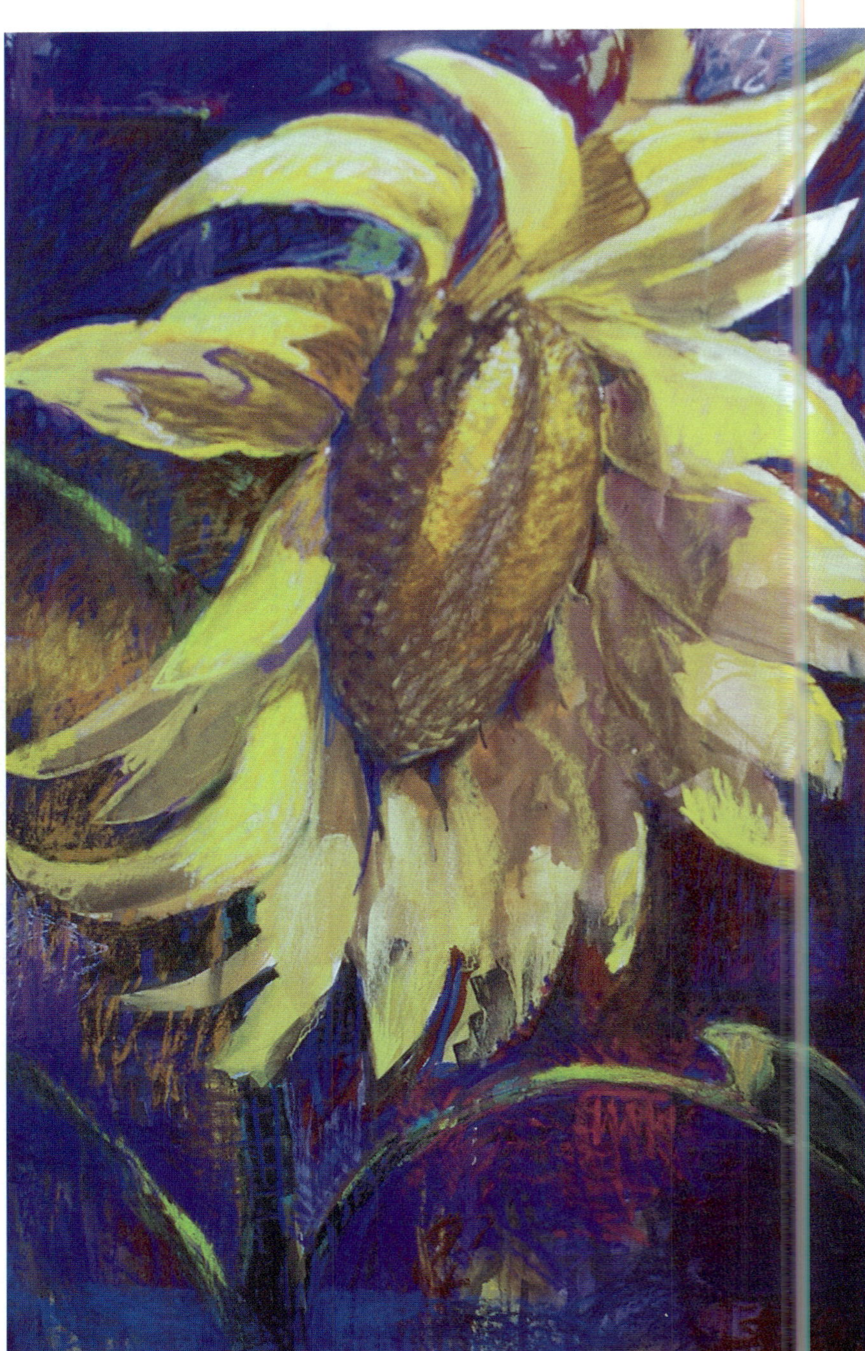

**SUNFLOWER I began this painting with rich, dark watercolor on a sanded paper. I could find no better way to maximize drama than with contrasts of light against dark, yellow against violet, and angular edges against a softer background. Compare the unblended strokes in this painting to the smooth strokes in the painting of the red ginger blossom. I also made the lighting on the sunflower almost strident in comparison, which really makes a dramatic impact on the the viewer.**

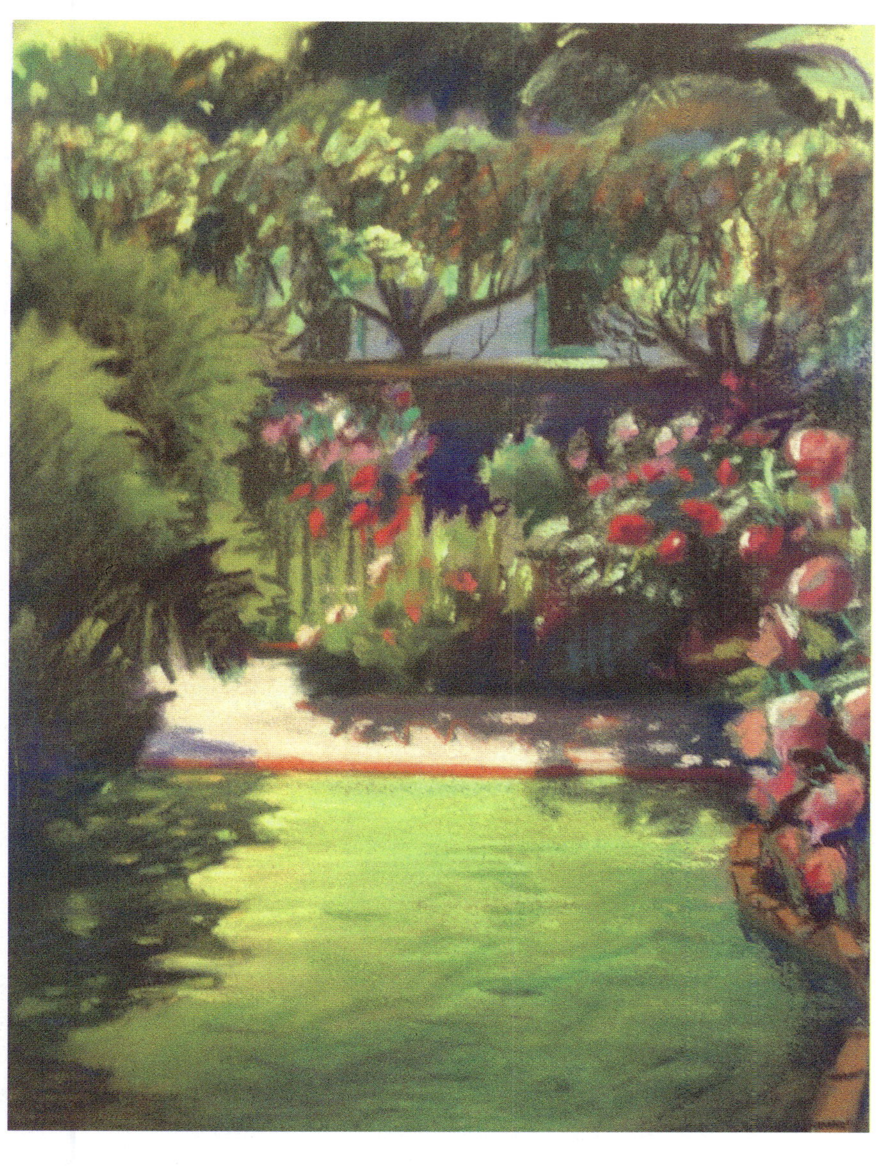

◄ **DEPICTING A GARDEN** The secret to painting a whole garden is to simplify the design to convey a sense of order. First I flattened the background trees and the hedge so they echoed the horizontal walkway, fence, and house. Then I carefully arranged the roses in clusters from large to small. Finally, I established a focal point on the left side of the lawn so the picture would not seem too "rose-heavy" on the right.

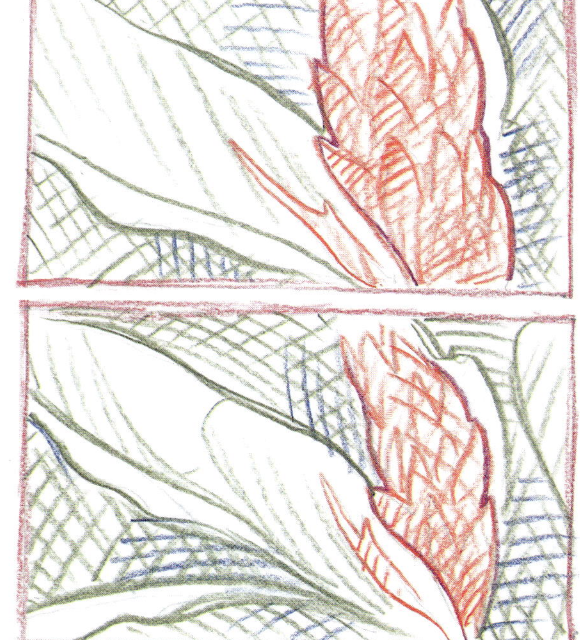

**FRAMING** I sketch different ways of framing a flower first, to find the best way to show it off.

### Displaying Flowers as Full-frame Compositions

When I have a particularly dramatic or exotic flower to paint, I like to make it so large that it commands immediate attention. This is the meaning of a "full-frame composition." You can use this technique to express a variety of feelings in your paintings. For example, in the sunflower painting on page 20, I used dynamic cropping and severe lighting to make a bold statement. *Red Ginger* is a more exotic flower, so I used color and light to evoke a sense of mystery (below).

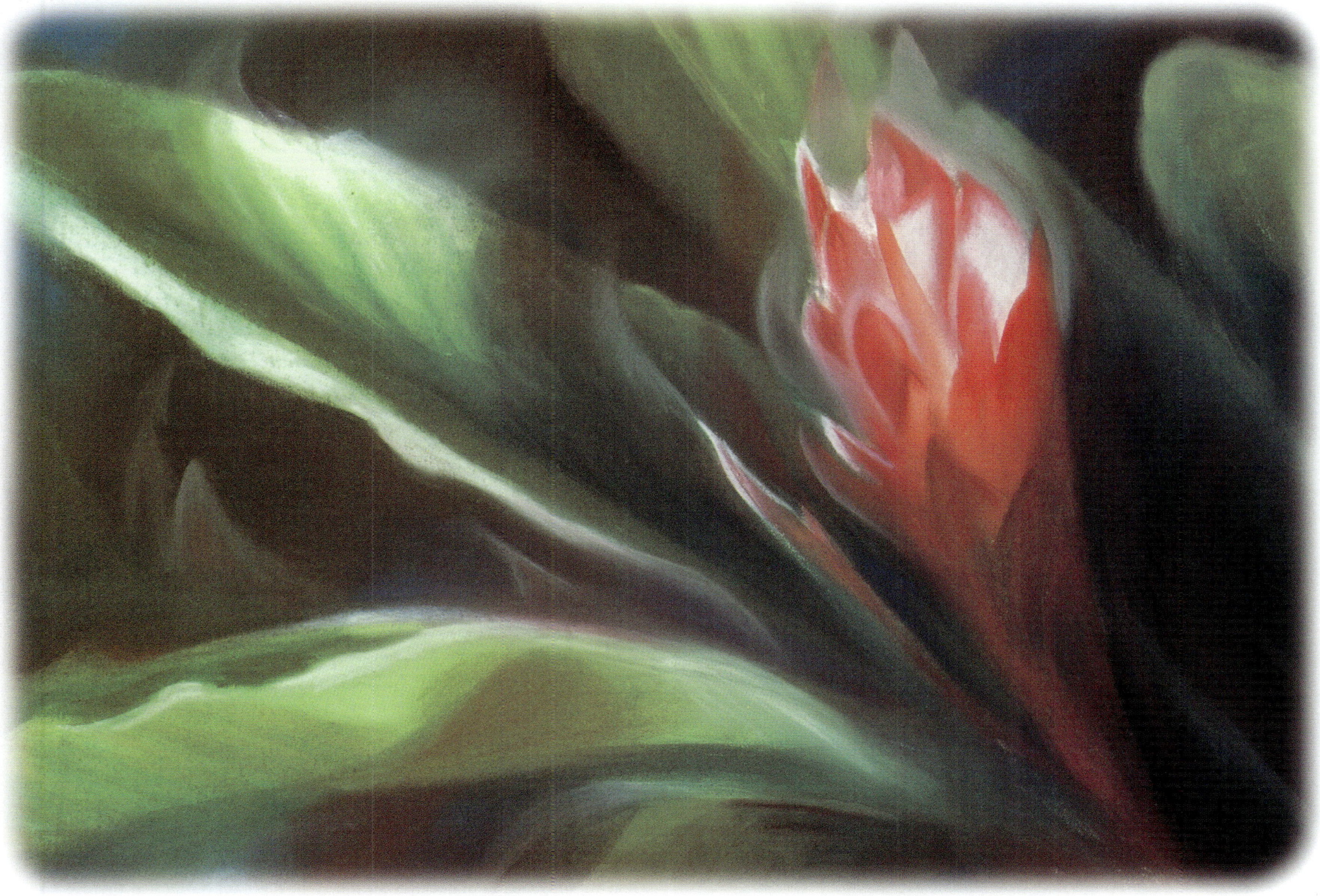

**RED GINGER** Here I made the light appear to come from within the flower, like an inner light, to create a mystical, exotic feeling.

# Combining Art and Architecture

BUILDINGS ARE A PERFECT SUBJECT for studying composition—the arrangement of elements and their size and shape relationships. Buildings are also wonderful for observing the effects of light, shadow, and reflected color on basic forms. When composing a painting of buildings, I always keep in mind that the most interesting compositions use diagonals to create a sense of movement, just as in my still lifes and interiors (see the discussion on pages 8 and 9). Good compositions also have a point of interest that's placed off-center, so the overall design isn't perfectly symmetrical. Let's take a closer look at the paintings on this page, and you'll see what I mean.

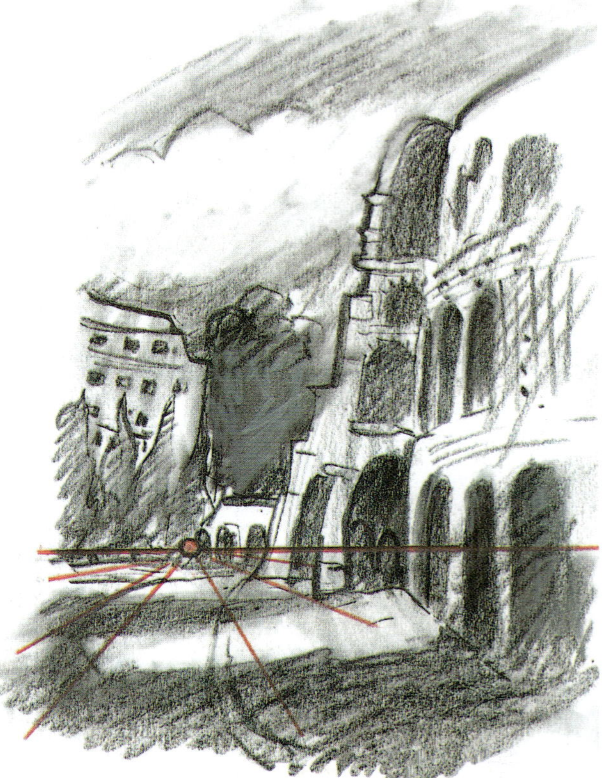

◄ **PLANNING THE COMPOSITION** **Before I start on a pastel, I sometimes make a quick thumbnail sketch to help me clarify the composition without worrying about drawing all the elements perfectly accurate. Here I worked out the perspective for *The Colosseum* (below), creating a definite foreground, middle ground, and background and using linear perspective (see page 6). I also tweaked the receding line of the road to the right, so my composition wouldn't be too symmetrical.**

### Creating Asymmetry

There's no real trick to making an asymmetrical composition; I just think about arranging things so everything isn't perfectly balanced. I particularly like playing around with the perspective when I paint buildings. I often take a somewhat exaggerated viewpoint, either by using an extreme left or right viewpoint or by raising or lowering the viewing angle, as shown in the architectural landscapes on these pages.

## Using a Viewfinder

When you're surveying a landscape or cityscape to paint, how do you decide which part to focus on? How do you zero in on a section that will make a good composition? One easy way is to look at the scene through a viewfinder. You can form a double "L" with your fingers or make a frame out of cardboard, as shown below, and check your composition by looking through the opening. Bring the viewfinder closer and hold it out farther; move it around the scene; look at your subject from high and low viewpoints. Then choose the view that works for you.

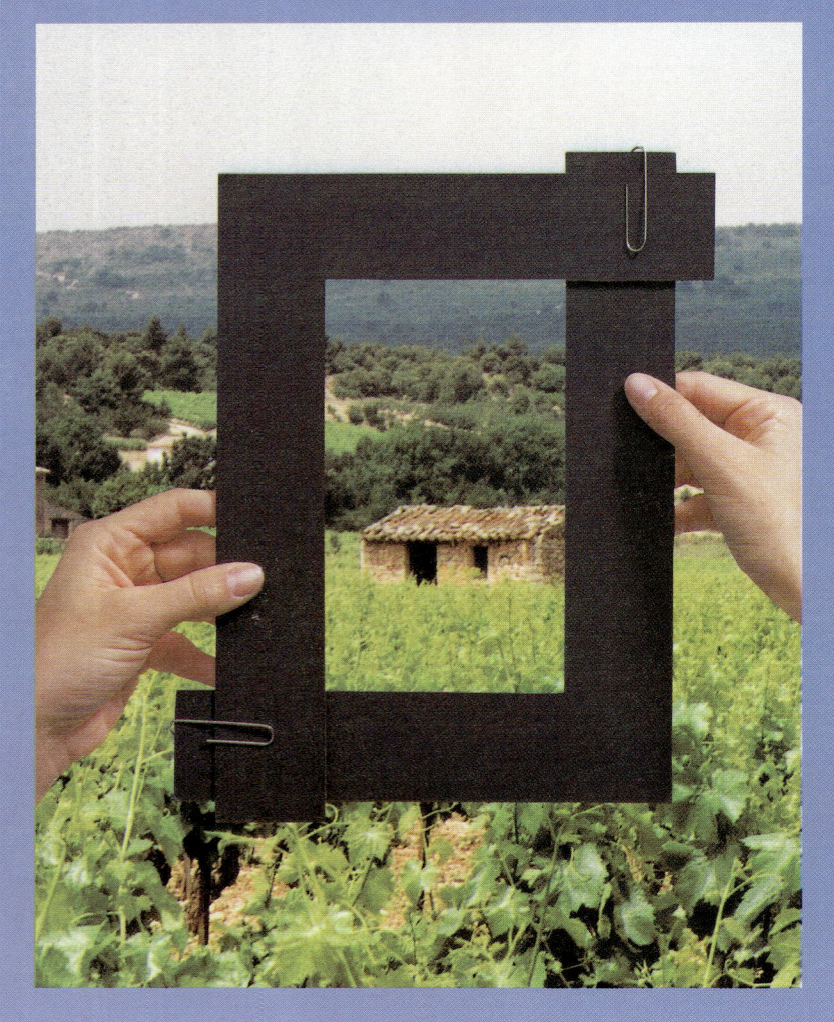

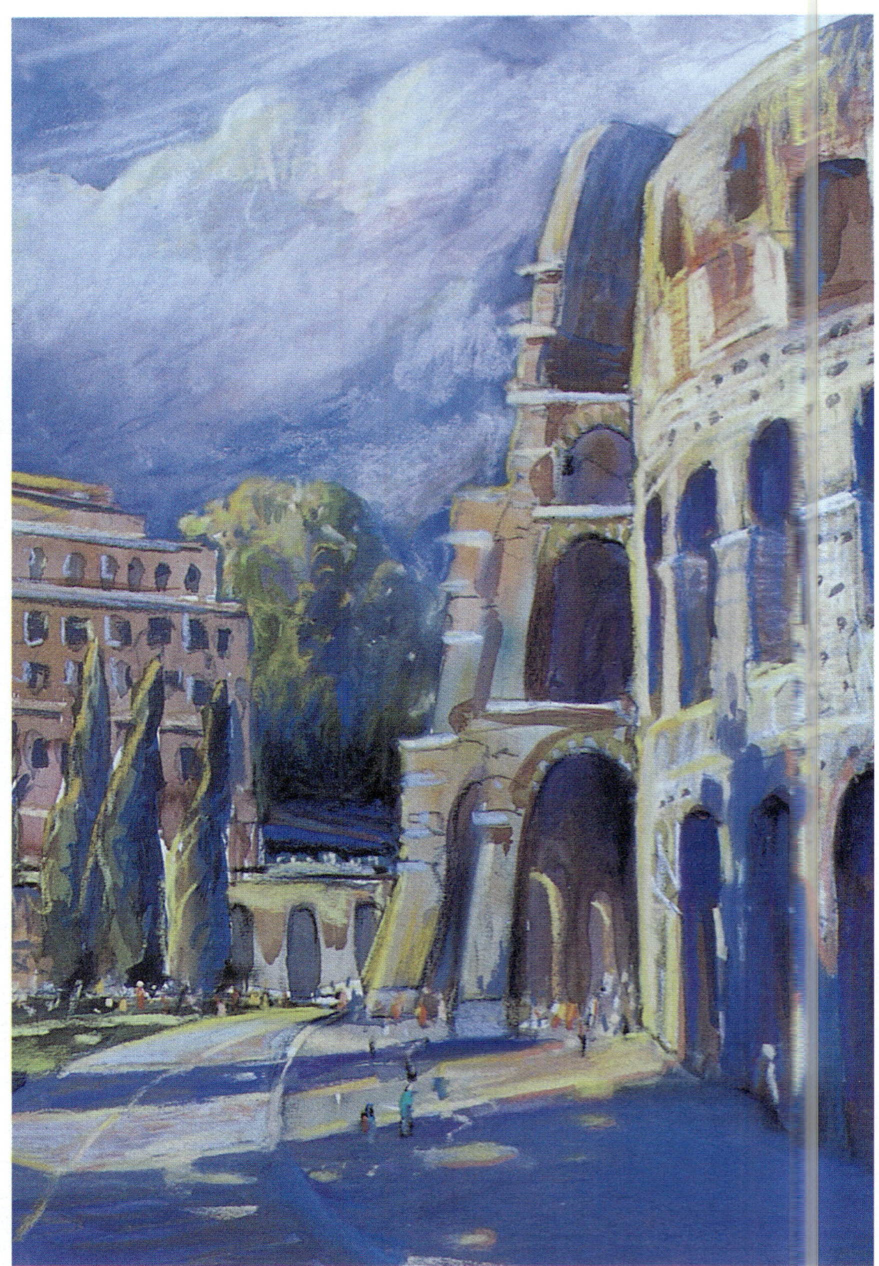

**APPLYING ASYMMETRY** **I placed the center of interest far to the right, leaving only the dark accents on the left and a strong foreground shadow to ease the viewer back into the picture. As the painting developed, I decided to invent a second shadow in the background so the eye could "follow the lines of perspective" and move deeper into the picture.**

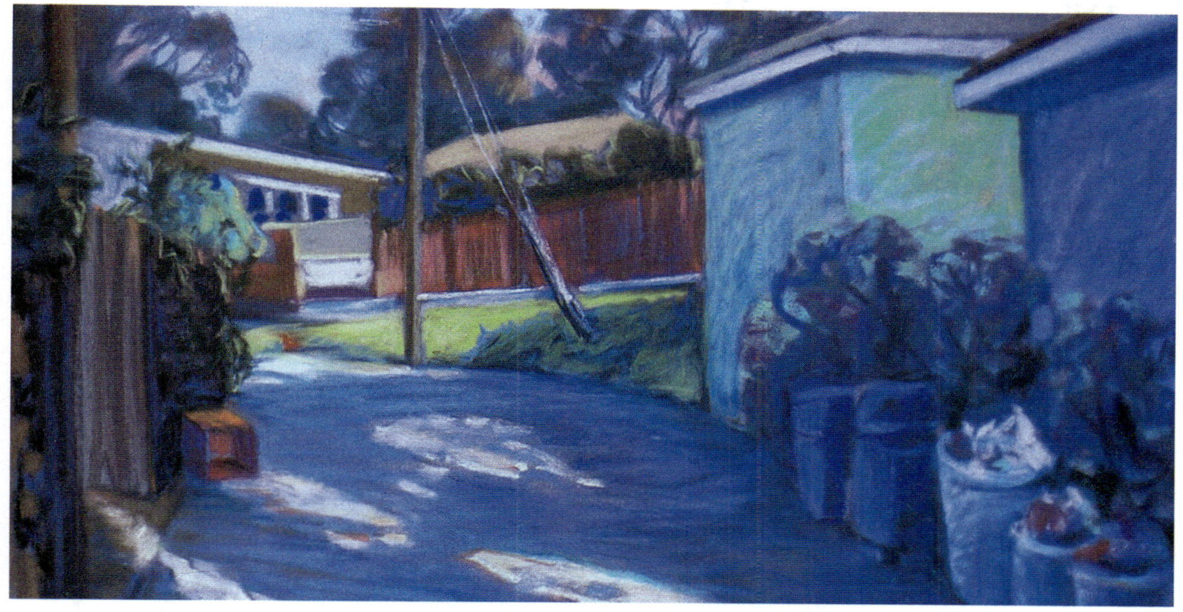

**CHOOSING UNUSUAL SUBJECTS** Alleys are great subjects to paint. They are usually quiet, and they often contain discarded objects with the most interesting shapes. Here I took a low viewpoint in order to lift up the focal point. This exposes more alleyway, giving me stronger, more interesting shadows. I especially like the way the row of trashcans plays "second fiddle" to the darker foreground garage and adds a subtle side note of personality to the alley.

## Utilizing Light and Color

In my travels, I am always on the lookout for areas that have a variety of architectural styles. I am especially drawn to older cities, such as in Greece, which often have buildings with curved arches, domes, and rounded sides. I approach painting a building as a collection of simple forms, such as spheres and cubes, being lit by a strong light source—the sun. I know that every form with a brightly lit side must also have a shadow side and a cast shadow. I also know that every cast shadow will contain some reflected color from the light that bounces back into the shadow. You can see this in the painting below. Although you'll have a hard time finding as perfect an example as this, the principle is universal and can be found anywhere.

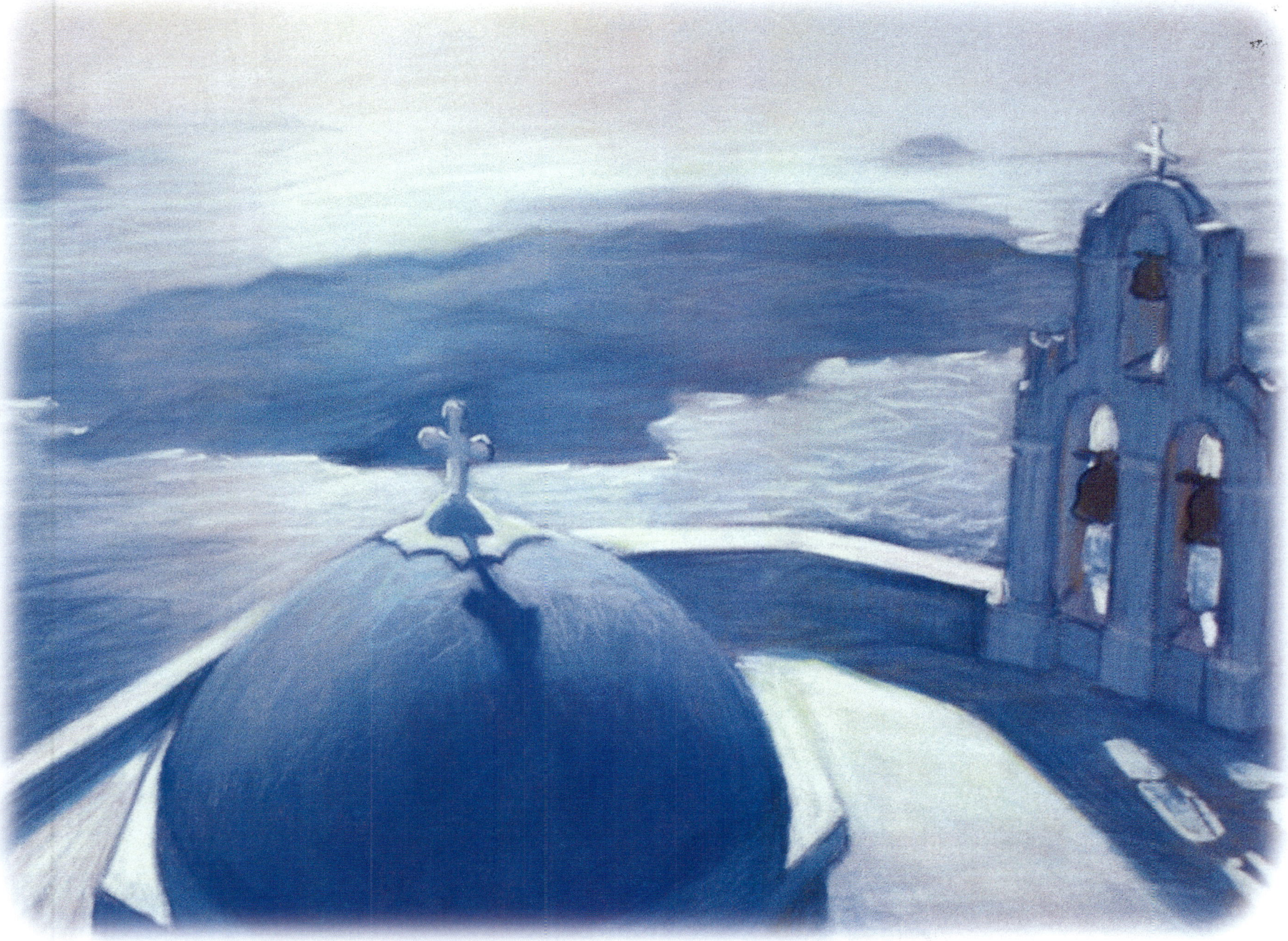

**CHANGING SHADOWS** Near an object, its cast shadow has hard edges, which soften as it lengthens. Also notice the reflected light visible in the shadow.

# Depicting Rivers and Seas

I LIKE TO THINK OF WATER on a windless day as a sheet of mirror that reflects the colors of the sky from zenith to horizon; it isn't just an expanse of solid blue. When water is agitated, it acts as if there were transparent chunks of glass imbedded in it. I can still see some reflection of the colors above the surface, but I can also see translucent ripples that reveal the deeper colors underneath. Many qualities of water are really fascinating to me, but here I will introduce you to a few of the properties that intrigue me the most.

## Analyzing Reflections on Moving Water

I often use the metaphor of moving water as containing shards of glass, or pieces of a mirror, to describe the way it seems to be broken into separate reflecting planes. When you look at moving water, you will see that light and color seem to skip around, dancing across its surface as if reflected by many pieces of mirror. In contrast, the darker ripples of water seem to hold transparent planes of glass tilted toward you, also catching light but showing you the colors under water, instead of reflecting the colors above. This is how I approach painting water and how I decide which colors to use where.

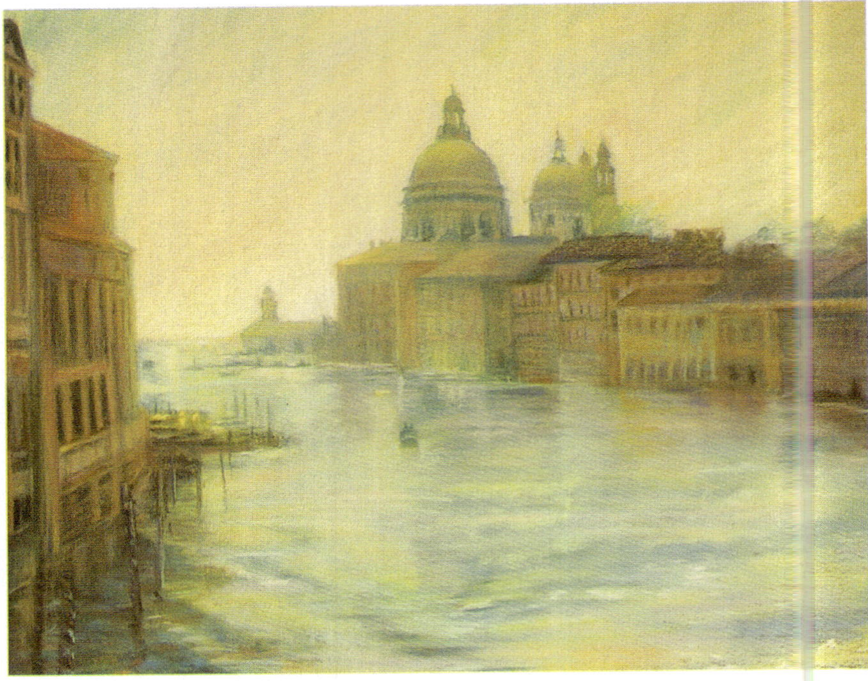

**SHOWING WATER IN MOTION** This painting of a waterway in Venice shows the way that light, color, and reflections break up across the surface when the water is moving, even if only slightly. Here I used short, choppy strokes and a lot of pale colors to create this effect.

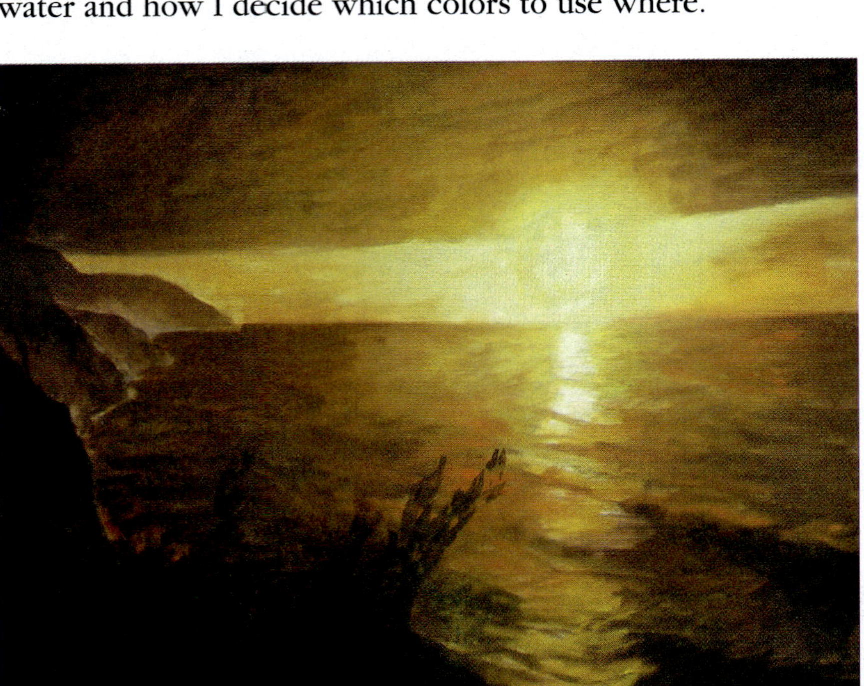

**SEEING COLORS** This painting shows another aspect of water that is often overlooked: Water isn't always blue. Here the orange-colored sky makes an orange-colored ocean. I started with an underpainting of raw umber watercolor and then blocked in the shapes with various brown pastels. I built up the painting with reds, oranges, and yellows, finishing with greens and blues in the foreground and around the edges for a cool contrast. Note how the light sparkles on the bushes accent the backlighting.

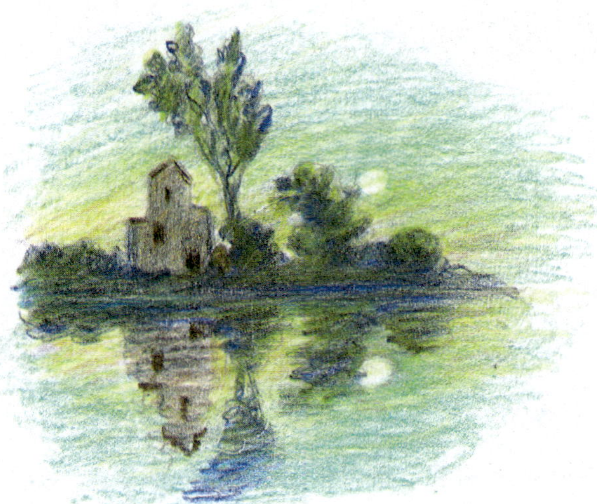

◄ **OBSERVING REFLECTIONS** When on location, I sometimes make quick colored pencil studies (like this one) to record the different shapes, colors, and values of the objects and their reflections.

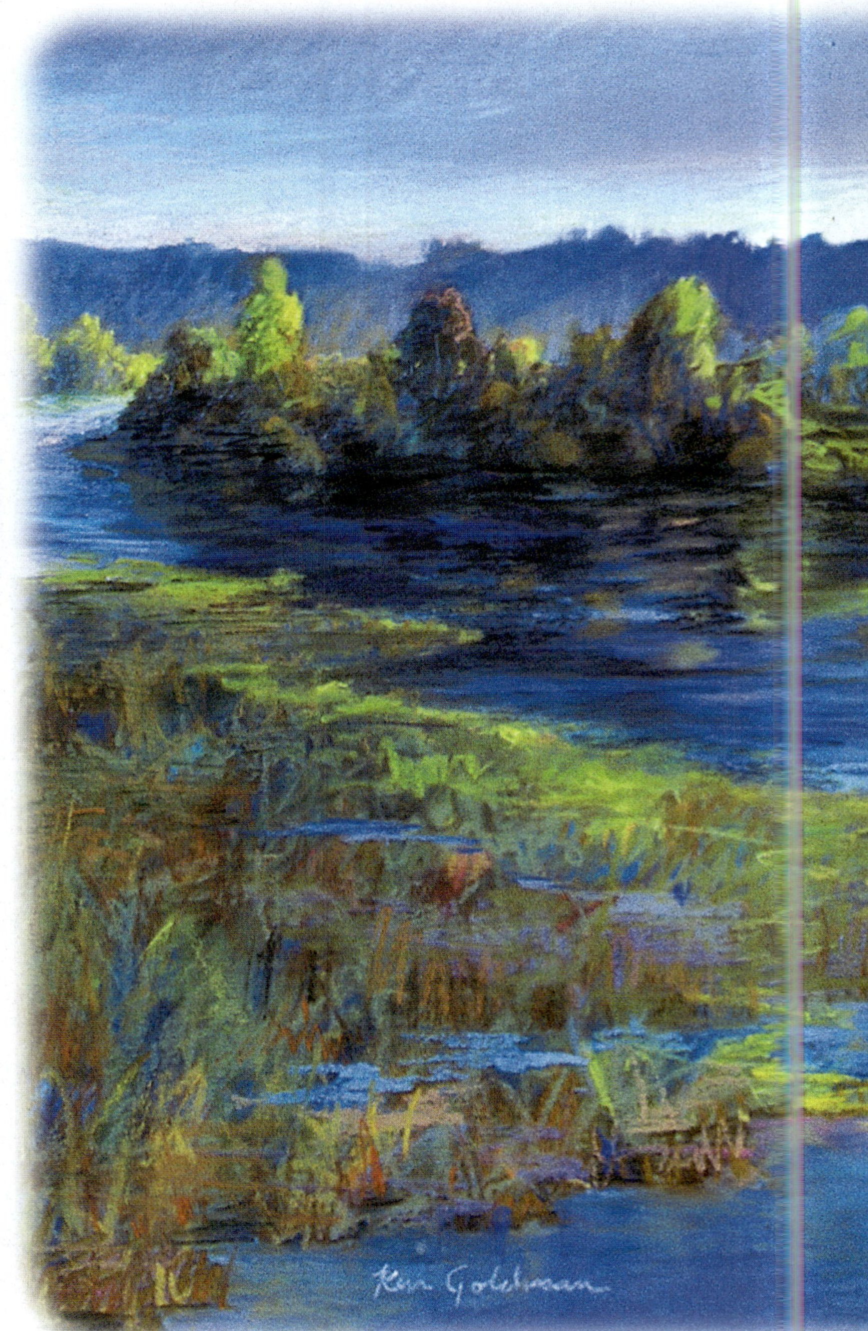

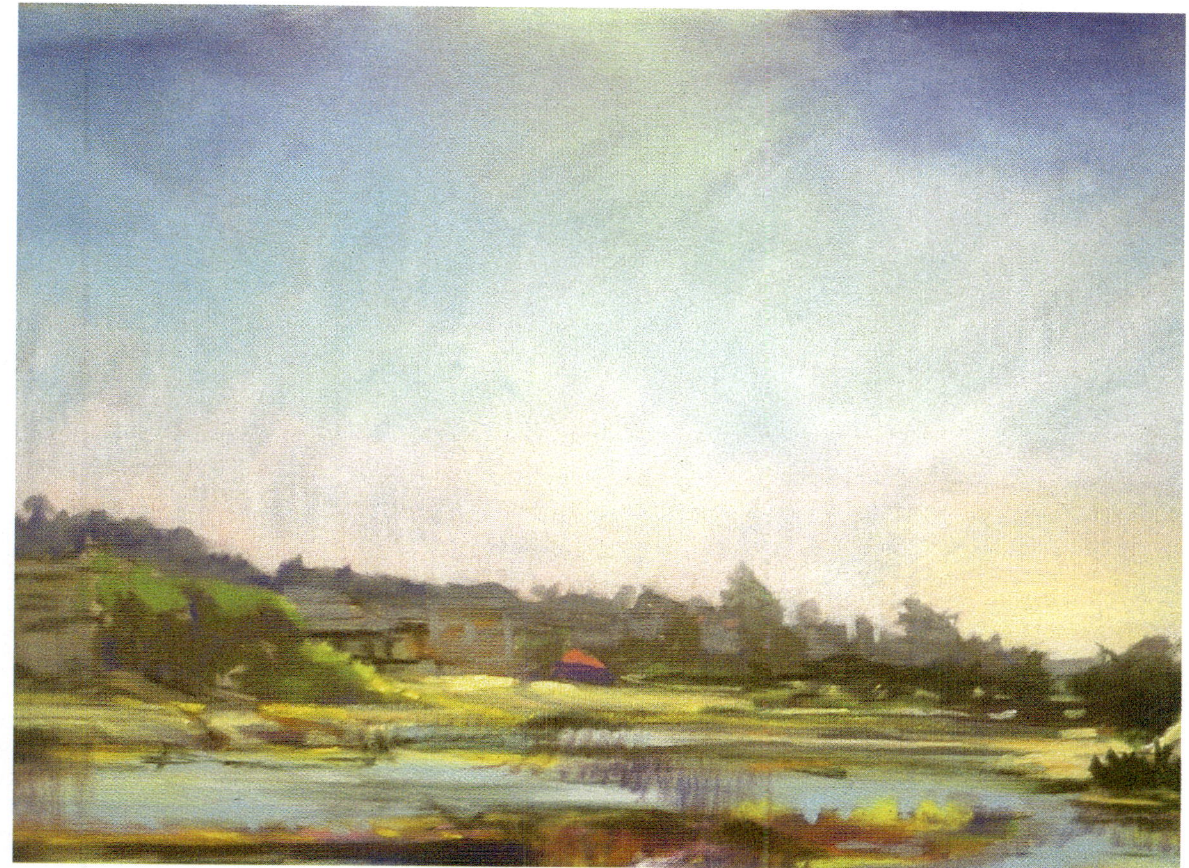

**PAINTING CALM WATER** This is an example of the way still water distinctly mirrors the image of the sky. If the water extended all the way to the horizon, the pinks in the sky would be reflected exactly. Similarly, if the water were more expansive in the foreground, you would also see the deep blue color of the sky directly above reflected on the water's glassy surface.

### Reflecting Images in Still Water

In water at rest, images are reflected the way a mirror reflects, but they aren't perfect replications. Here are some "rules" about reflections that will help you paint them. First, in reflections, colors will be "flattened," or not so intense. Also, light-colored objects will appear somewhat darker, and dark-colored objects will appear a bit lighter. Finally, an object's form won't appear as crisp and distinct in reflections. You can see this aspect in my painting of the slough at left and in the reflections of the trees in the San Diego River scene below.

**Artist's Tip**

*It is easier to show the water's depths when you take a view at a steep angle. What looks brownish up close will appear sky-colored from an angle.*

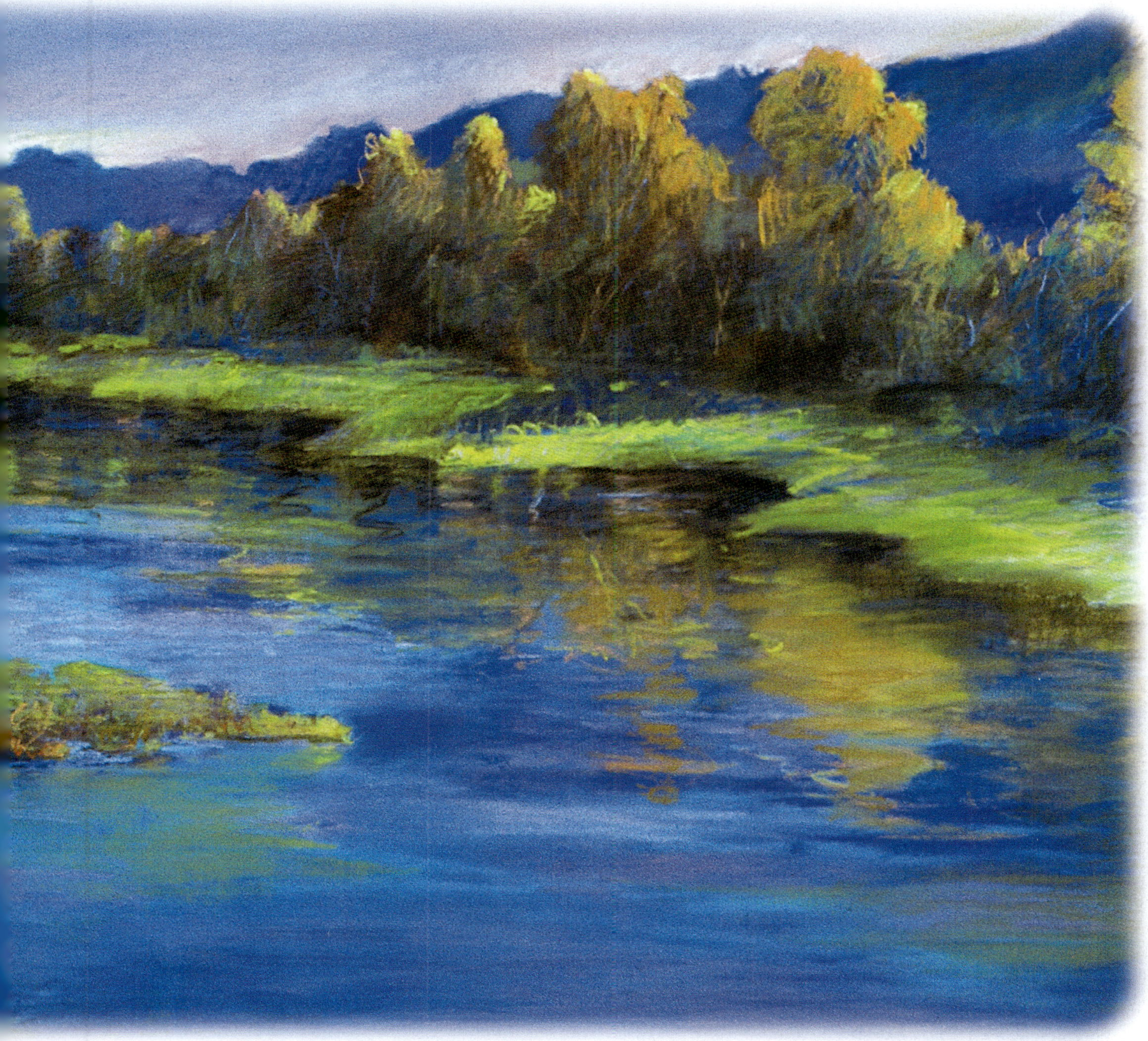

◄ **RENDERING REFLECTIONS** In this painting of a river, you can clearly see how I softened the edges of the trees' reflections. Although I used the same colors for their mirrored images, I chose much brighter tones of oranges and greens for the actual trees. I also showed reflections of the pinks and blues of the sky and distant hills; they appear broken up because the current created ripples on the water's surface. To complement the watery theme, I painted this pastel over a watercolor base of darks. Then I built up many of the foreground forms using crosshatched strokes of both pure color and gray hard pastels.

# Developing a Portrait

I BELIEVE THAT PORTRAITURE is one of the most rewarding areas of study in art. It's also all-encompassing. The human face in its simplest form contains all the geometric shapes found in any other subject, and painting it is just a matter of applying the few simple basics of drawing, color, value, and lighting described elsewhere in this book. With a little practice in those areas, you'll be well prepared for trying your hand at portraiture. And once you have learned the secrets of painting portraits, painting landscapes, still lifes, and wildlife will seem even easier than before!

## Painting Skin Tones

Not all skin tones are alike, but in the examples below I offer some fairly standard "formulas" you can use for light, medium, and dark complexions, respectively. Light-colored flesh tones are made up of strokes of light red (pink), yellow, light green, and white. The red and green intermix through crosshatching and flat strokes, as shown in the swatch below. Medium complexions can be painted with light green, light pink, and light gray. Dark complexions are composed mostly of dark red (burnt sienna), medium yellow (raw sienna), and medium green (sap green). Depending on how much white is added, these colors form the basis for medium-dark to dark skin tones. To enrich the shadows on dark skin, try adding a little blue or purple.

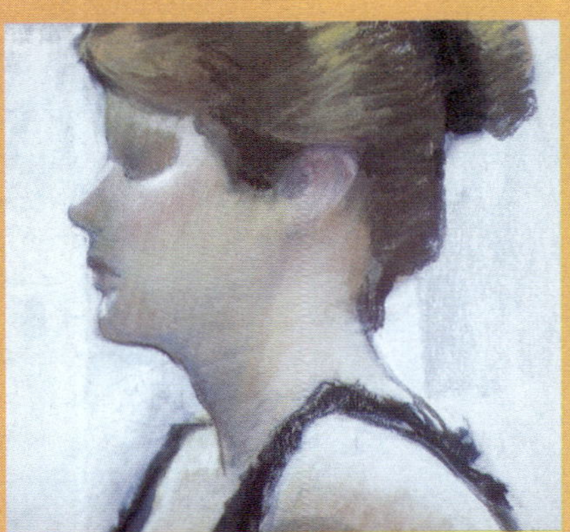

*Light skin tones: Cadmium red light, light green, and yellow with white*

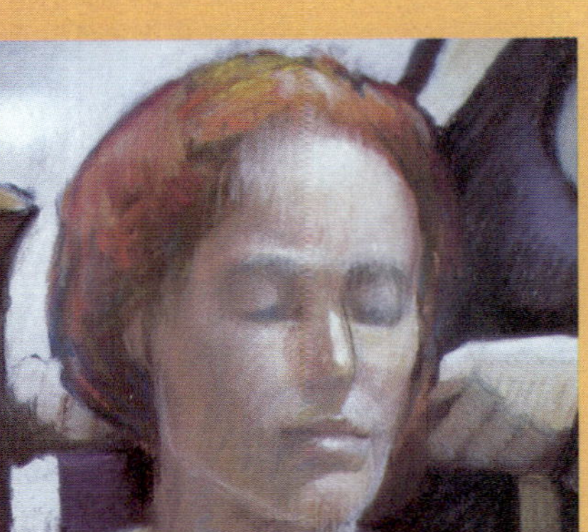

*Medium skin tones: Light green, light gray, and light pink*

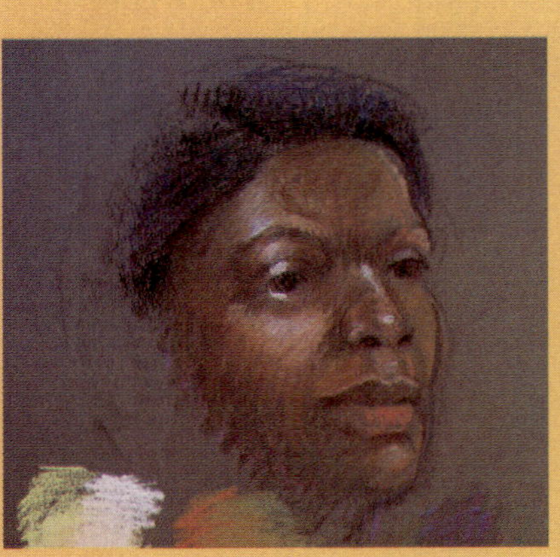

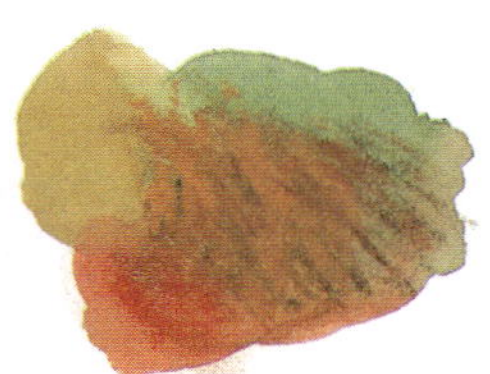

*Dark skin tones: Dark red, yellow ochre, and dark green*

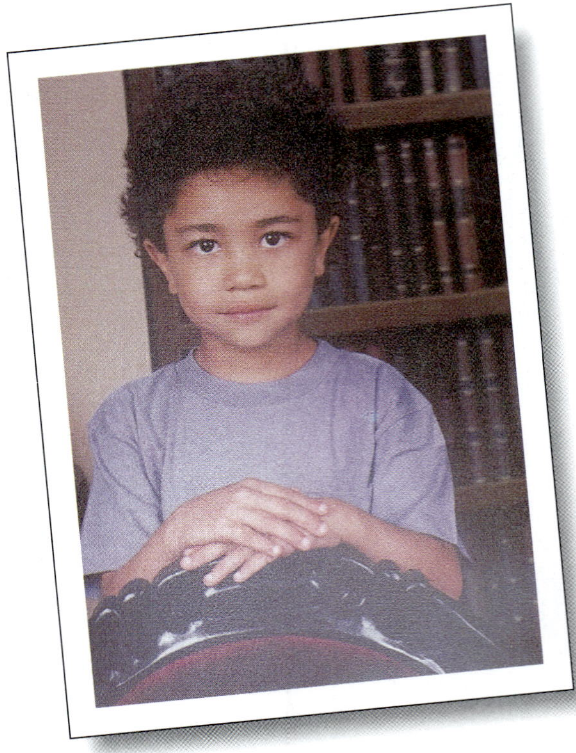

**◂ WORKING FROM A PHOTO** Children normally can't sit still long enough to pose, so I often set up a photo session and take at least one roll of slides, using a strong directional light. Flash photography makes the subject a little flat (as you can see in this photo).

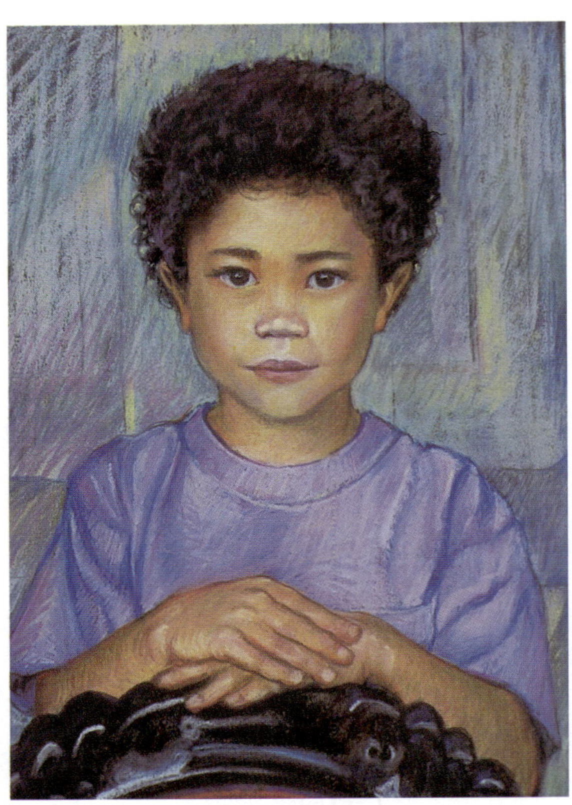

**◂ BRINGING OUT THE COLORS** Comparing this portrait to the photo, you can see how I intensified the colors, altered the background and darkened the shadows on the side of Karim's head. For this portrait, I chose green pastel paper and used hard pastels for the most part. I painted his skin tones using mostly yellow ochre, red, and a touch of light green for the shadows. Then I blended his face with my finger and left the background rough for contrast.

### Capturing a Likeness

Creating a likeness of a person comes from carefully copying the shapes, values, and colors you see. It takes some practice, but I can help you simplify matters. I recommend that beginners work from a photo turned upside down; this will help you paint what you really see, rather than following some preconceived notions about how to render people. Second, approach a portrait as you would any subject: break the image down into simple shapes; then refine them with details. Finally, remember that all skin tones, regardless of a person's race, are variations in lights and darks of red mixed with yellow-orange and with similar values of green or blue (see box at left).

### Lighting a Portrait

Lighting involves more than choosing a light source. Lighting also has a tremendous effect on the strength of the values and on creating a focal point in your portraits. I have found that the best way to learn about lighting, values, and focal point in portraiture is to work from a photo with a strong light source and to use a limited palette, as I have done with the portrait shown at right.

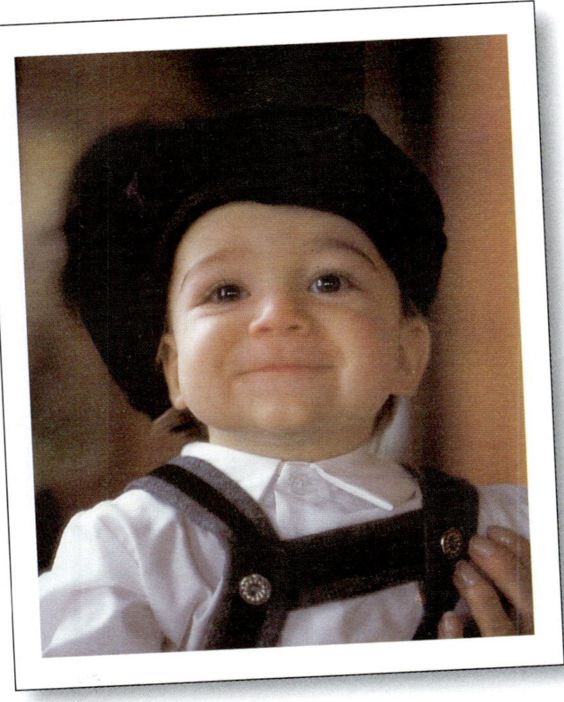

◄ **CHOOSING A VIEWPOINT** Part of Jacob's perky expression comes from his pose, which I captured by viewing him from below eye level. See how the ear lobes line up below the mouth rather than with the nose, as they would if they were viewed at eye level.

► **ALTERING ELEMENTS** I was asked to create a different background for this portrait. It is often necessary to make the composition more interesting and show off the subject to his or her best advantage.

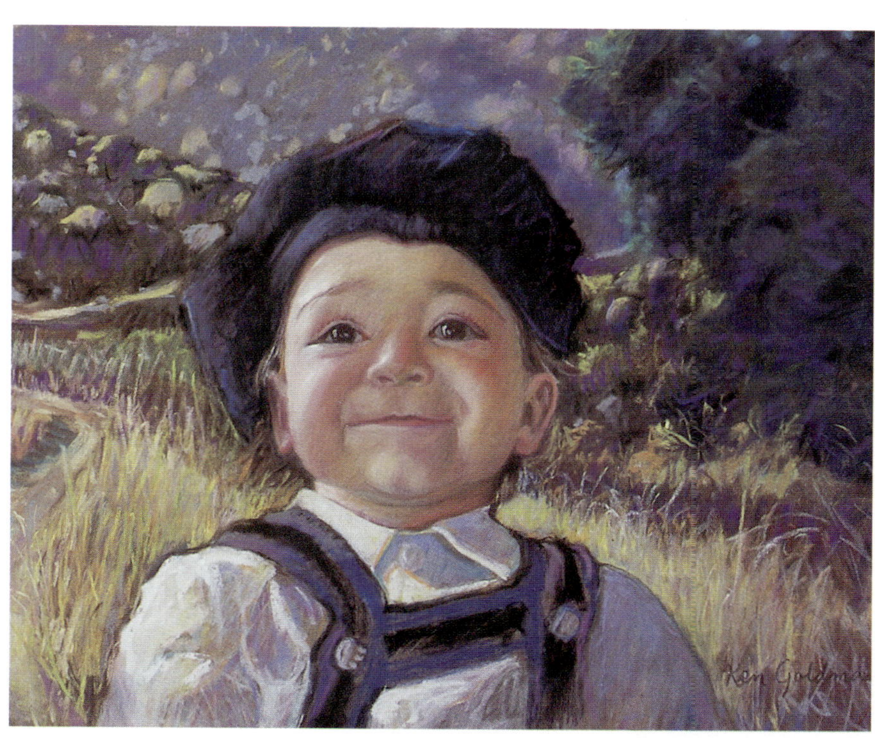

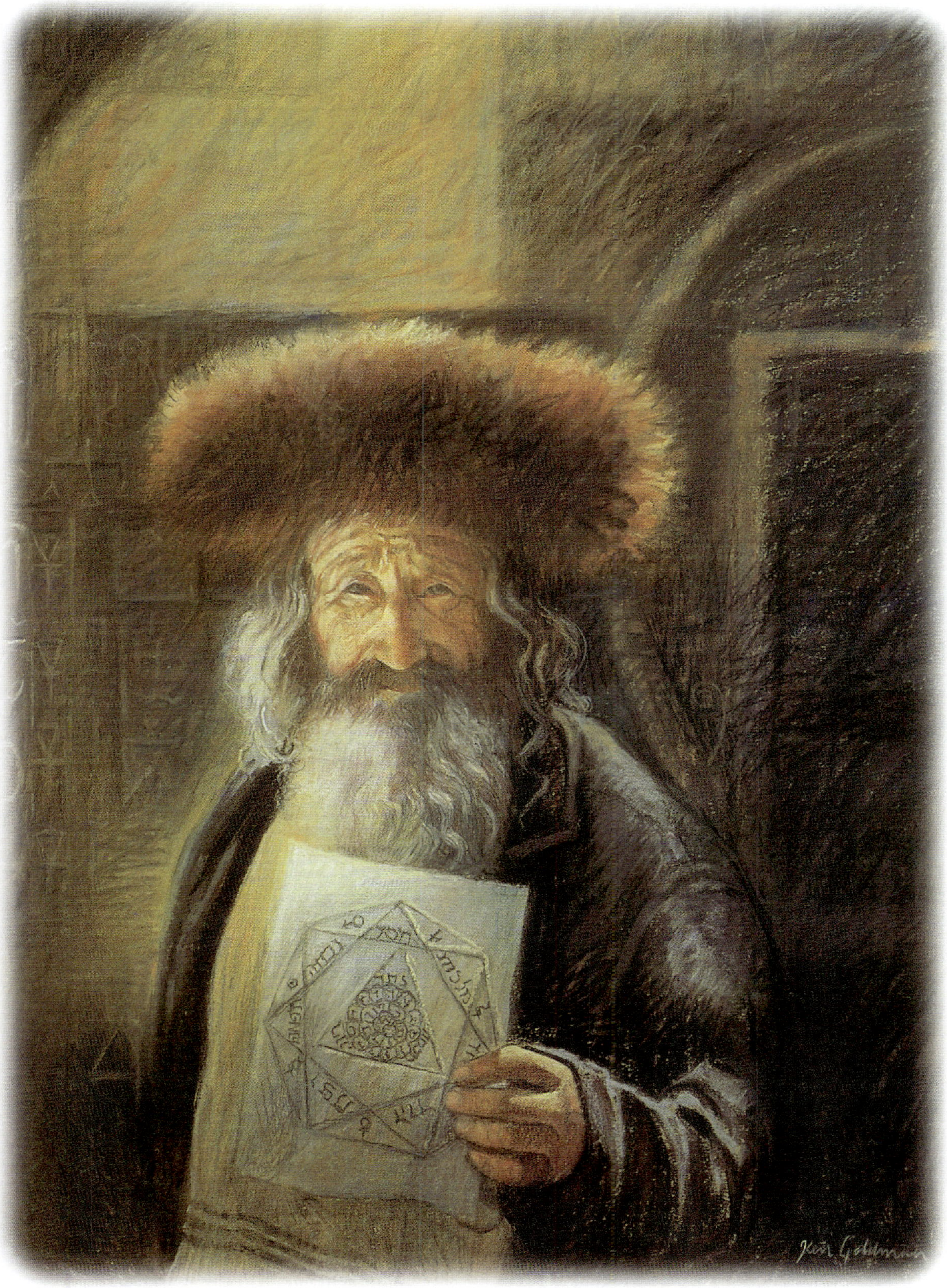

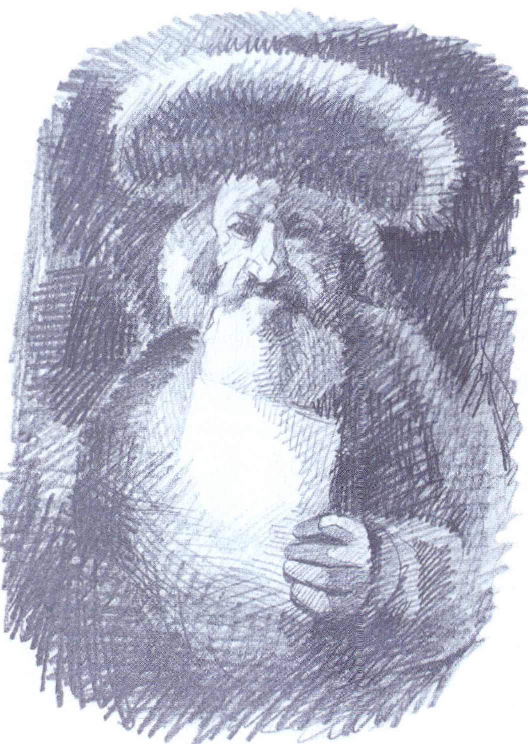

▲ **STUDYING VALUES** I worked out the dramatic lighting for my painting in this pencil study. Here the light source is primarily from the left, establishing three main values. Notice that I put the lightest values only where I wanted the focus to be—on the rabbi's face, letter, and hand.

◄ **USING A LIMITED PALETTE** With just a few colors—dark cool gray, dark burnt sienna, raw sienna, and white—I was able to capture this rabbi's essential character. I added detail and highlights only on areas I considered important for conveying his personality.

# Putting It All Together

PAINTING A PICTURE IS A PROCESS that does not always go as planned, so perfectionism is one of the greatest pitfalls for a beginning artist. Paintings take time, and solutions sometimes come when you least expect them. A teacher of mine once told me, "Don't try to make it perfect; just make it better and better each time." This teacher also told me to take breaks often, look at my work upside down, use a mirror to gain fresh perspectives, and step back as often as possible. Beginners think stepping back is a distraction; professionals know it is essential. Now that you have the best advice I can give, test it all out for yourself, and decide what works for you.

All the elements in this book can be summarized as follows: Everything is made of light, color, value, shape, and design. Eliminate your conceptions of what is beautiful or ugly, and all is fair game. Remember that lovely patterns of light, shadow, color, and form can be found as easily in alleys as in pastoral scenes. Just keep looking around you, and you will never want for subjects to paint. To help you keep the essentials in mind, I've assembled the following six short "tips for success," illustrated with details from my painting on page 31. Post this chart by your easel when you paint, and you'll never go wrong. Good luck, and happy painting!

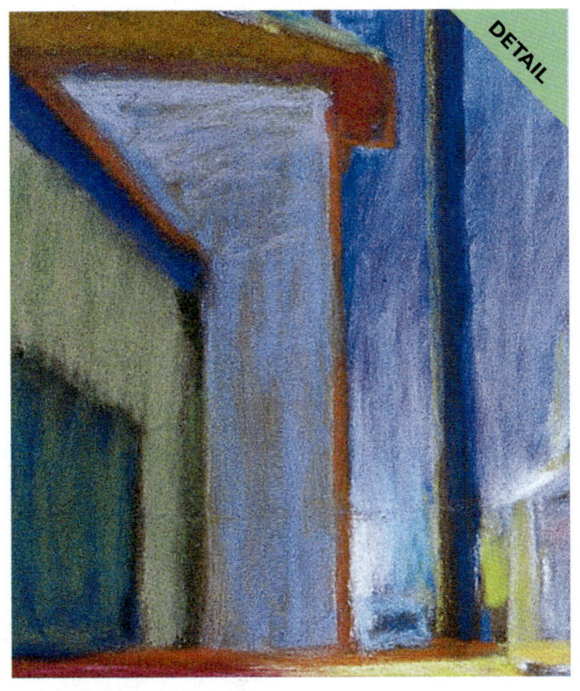


**1. KEEP IT SIMPLE** Keep your images as simple as possible, and paint the easiest things first. Minimize the number of values and colors you use, so you will have a more focused subject. Here I started with the simple geometric shapes of the buildings and used a limited palette.

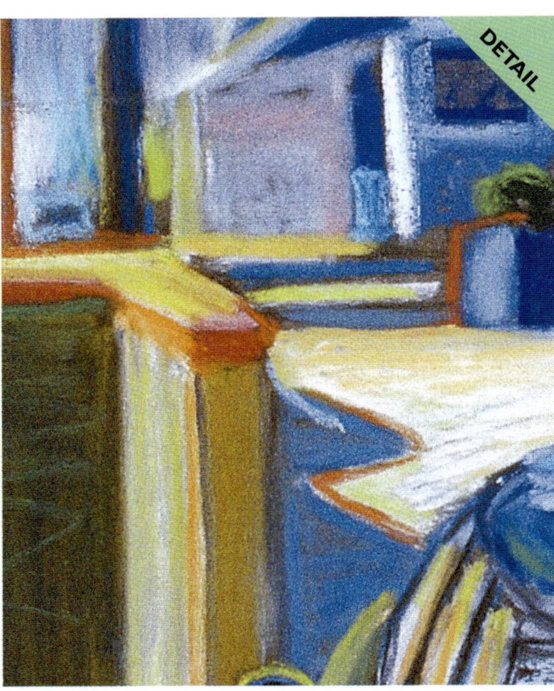


**2. START WITH CHANGEABLES** Finish what may change right away. The sun was hitting the street quite strongly, and I knew it wouldn't be long before the sun moved and altered the way the light hit. Assess what is likely to change, and attend to it first. Save what stays still for later.

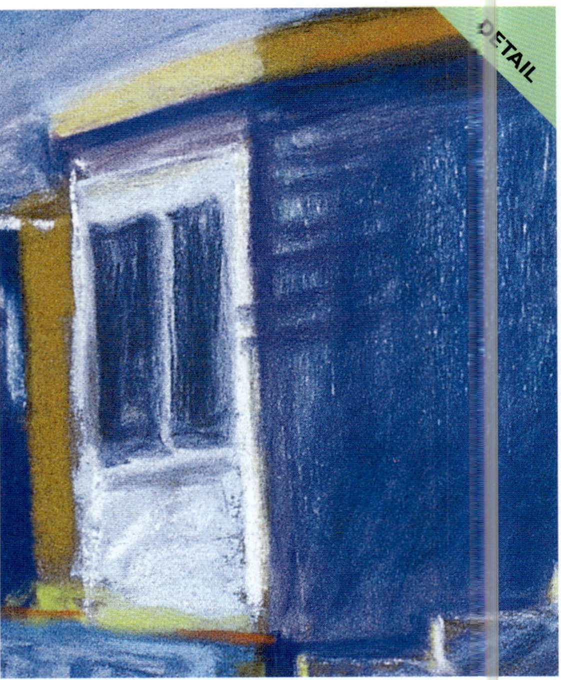


**3. LIGHT ISN'T WHITE** It's color. Eliminate the white of your paper by toning it right away, or use a toned paper instead. I chose a gray-toned paper for this painting, and I used mixes of yellows and blues for the lightest parts of the buildings, saving pure white (or nearly pure) for the highlights.

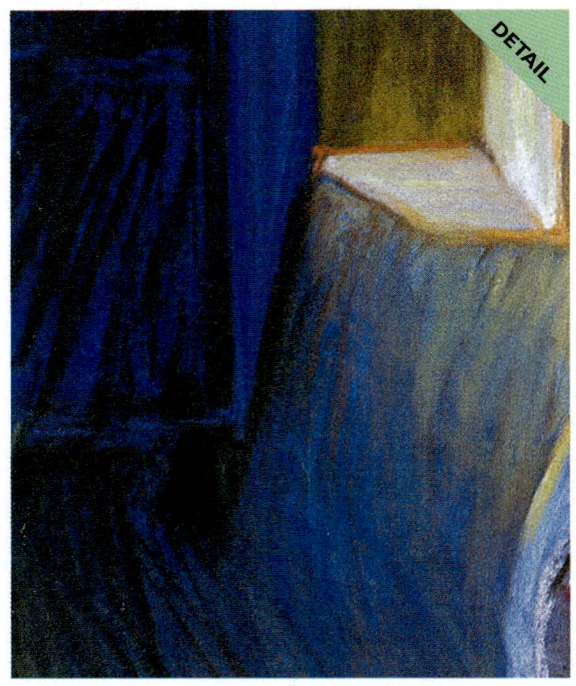


**4. DON'T MAKE SHADOWS TOO DARK** Start painting shadows with a middle tone, so the dark and light accents will have impact. They can always be darkened later if necessary. After painting the lights over the midtones, I added black to make this the darkest area of the whole painting.

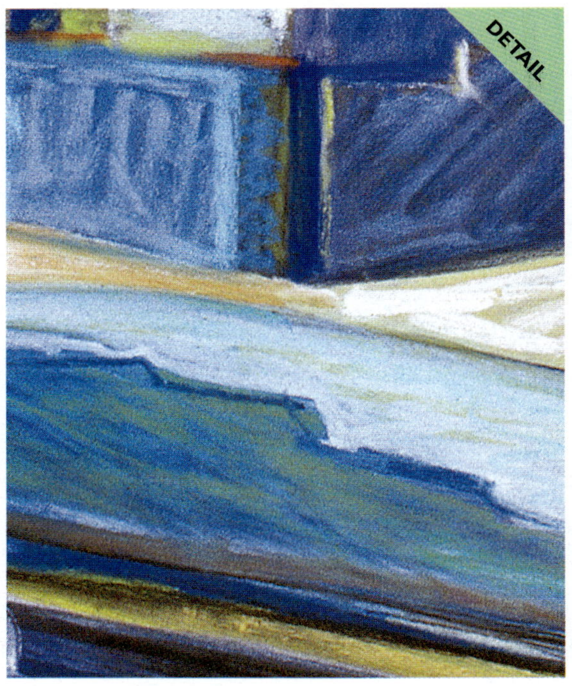


**5. SEE LIGHTS AND SHADOWS AS SHAPES** Try to paint the light and shadow areas objectively by looking at their actual shapes and then duplicating those shapes on your paper. Instead of thinking of this as the roof of the car, I painted what I saw: two irregular shapes of light and dark.

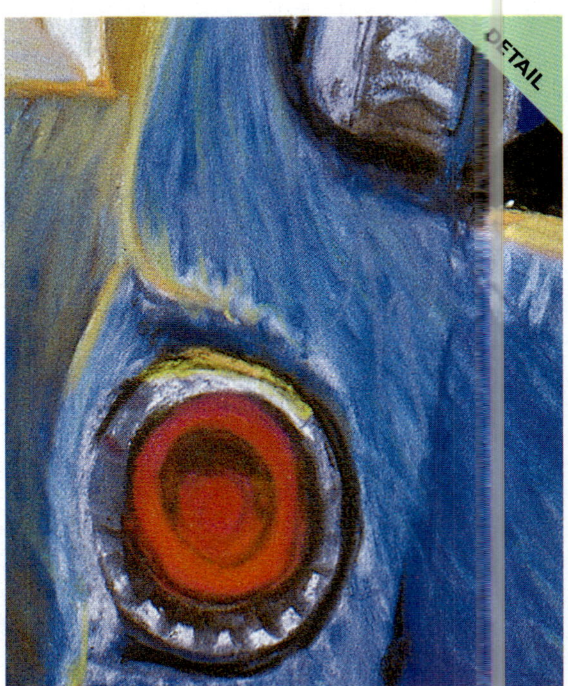


**6. THINK "CONTRAST"** Use contrasts of shape, form, size, texture, and especially color. Here I made this hot-red taillight really pop by setting it within a sea of cool, cool blue—and notice the orange accents. Remember, surround a color with its complement, and it really sparkles!

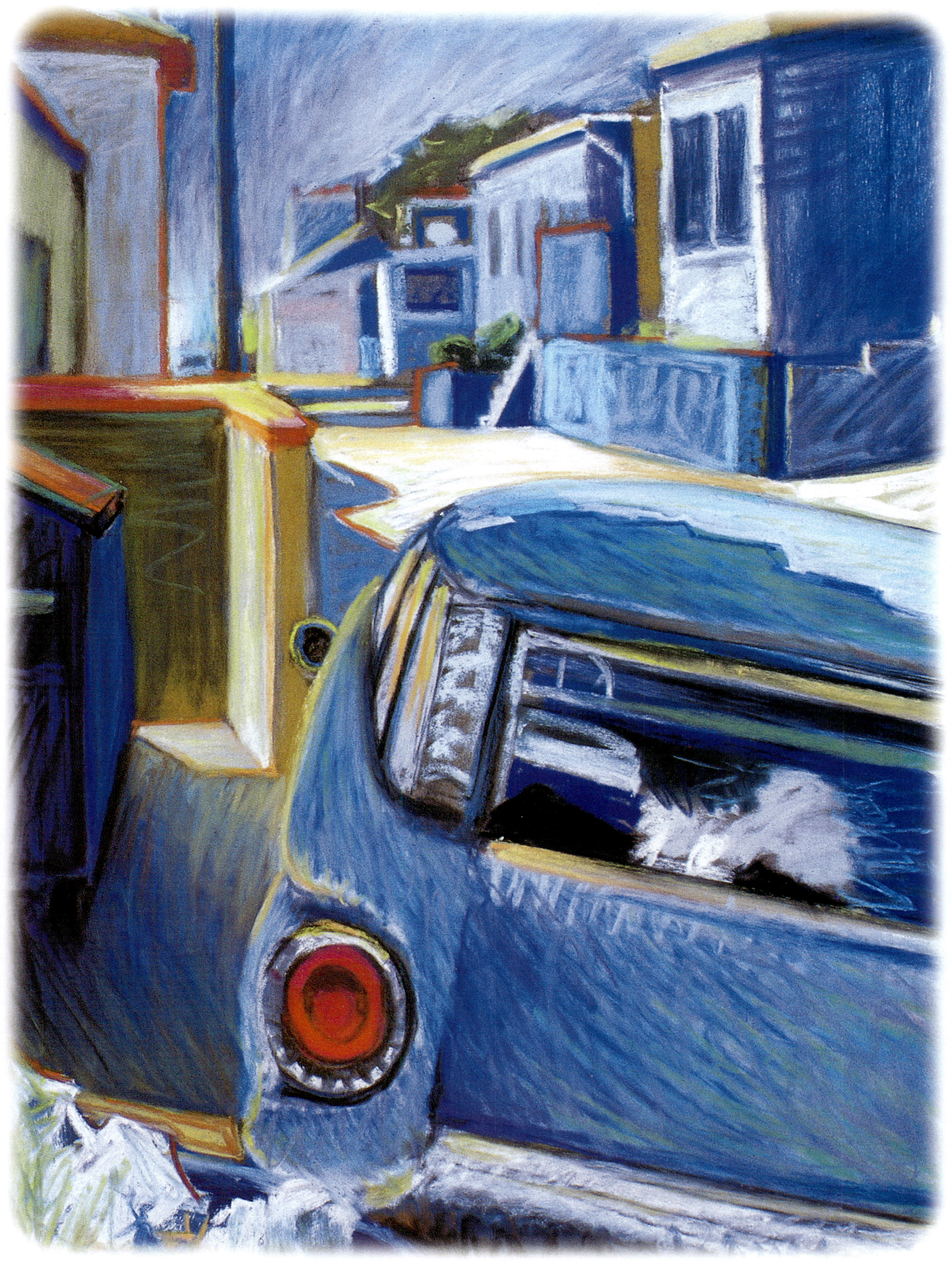

**MY FALCON** This painting is a study in light and shadow, value and tone, and contrasts of every kind—all six tips at work!

# More Ways to Learn

## Artist's Library

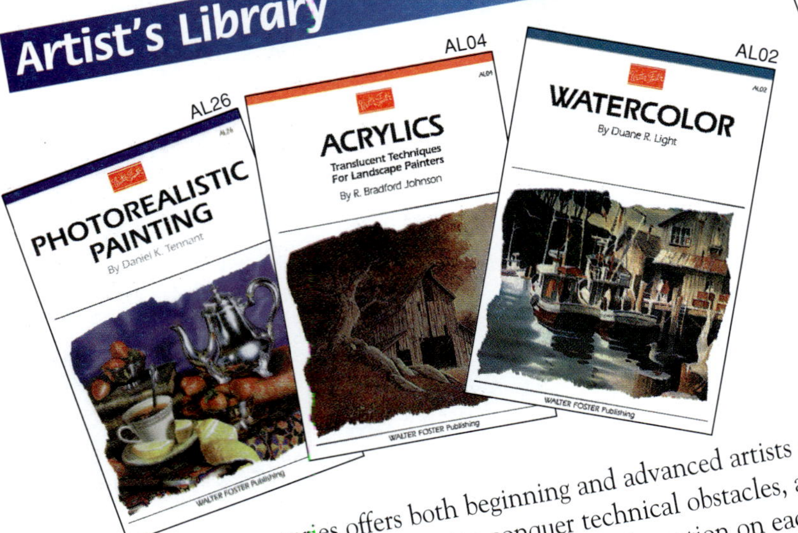


The **Artist's Library** series offers both beginning and advanced artists many opportunities to expand their creativity, conquer technical obstacles, and explore new media. You'll find in-depth, thorough information on each subject or art technique featured in the book. Each book is written and illustrated by a well-known artist who is qualified to help take eager learners to a new level of expertise.

*Paperback, 64 pages, 6-1/2" x 9-1/2"*

## Collector's Series

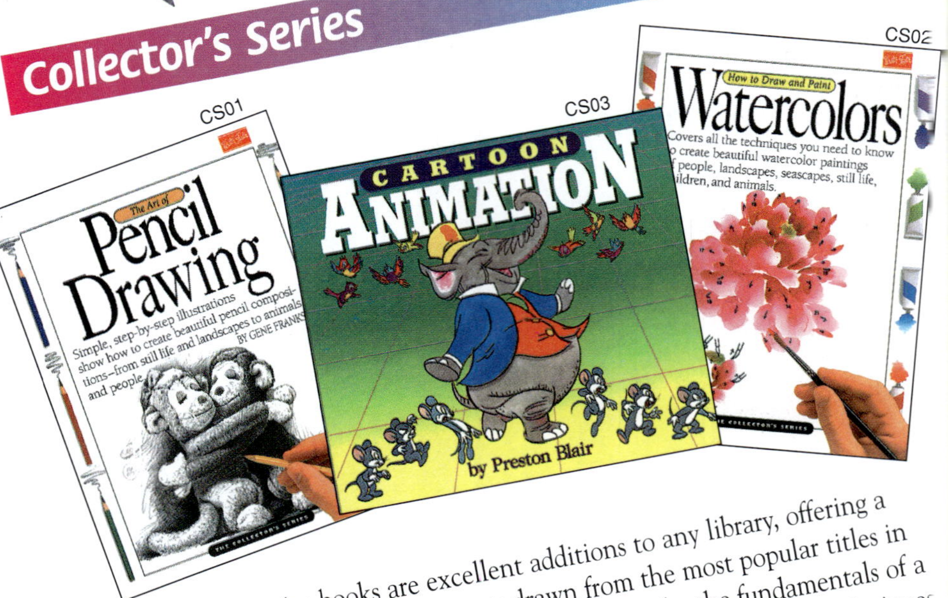


**Collector's Series** books are excellent additions to any library, offering a comprehensive selection of projects drawn from the most popular titles in our How to Draw and Paint series. These books take the fundamentals of a particular medium, then further explore the subjects, styles, and techniques of featured artists.

*CS01, CS02, CS04: Paperback, 144 pages, 9" x 12"*
*CS03: Paperback, 224 pages, 10-1/4" x 9"*

## How to Draw and Paint

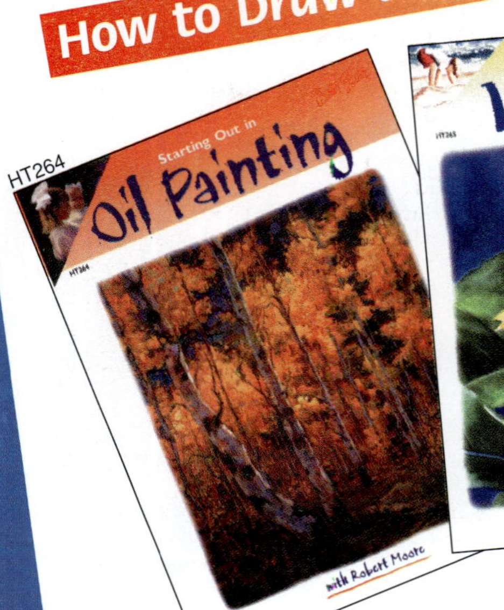


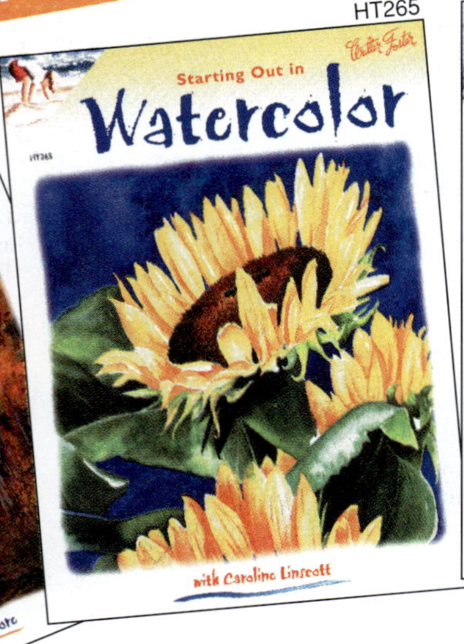


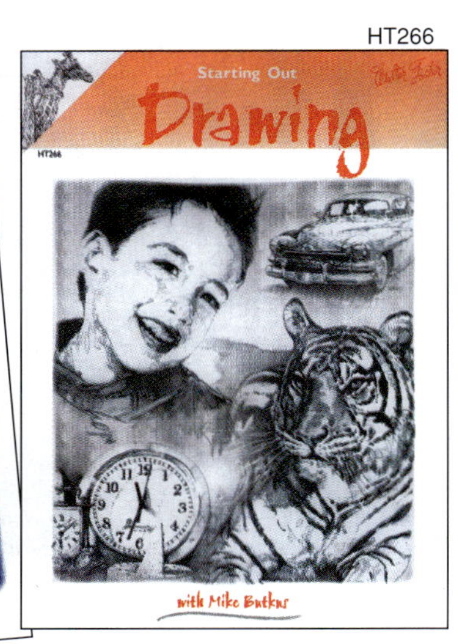


HT268 Starting Out in Pastel

Step-by-Step Watercolor

The **How to Draw and Paint** series includes these five stunning new titles to enhance an extensive collection of books on every subject and medium to meet any artist's needs. Specially written to encourage and motivate, these new books offer essential information in an easy-to-follow format. Lavishly illustrated with beautiful drawings and gorgeous art, this series both instructs and inspires.

*Paperback, 32 pages, 10-1/4" x 13-3/4"*



Walter Foster Publishing, Inc. • 23062 La Cadena Drive • Laguna Hills, CA 92653 • (800) 426-009